GW01236595

Mrs Houblon's
Side-Saddle

MRS ARCHER HOUBLON, C.V.O., *riding* "IMPERIAL".
From the painting by Terence Cuneo. Reproduced by Gracious Permission of H.M. The Queen

Mrs Houblon's
Side-Saddle

Revised and Updated by
Sylvia Stanier
L.V.O.

Foreword by
Sir John Miller
K.C.V.O., D.S.O., M.C.

With a 4-colour frontispiece and 42 black-and-white
illustration plates

J. A. Allen
London

British Library Cataloguing in Publication Data

Houblon, Doreen Archer
   Side-saddle.—Rev. ed.
   1. Sidesaddle riding
   I. Title   II. Stanier, Sylvia
   798.2'3   SF309.27

ISBN 0-85131-409-0

First published, in 1938, as *Side-Saddle*.
Revised 1950 and 1973. Reprinted 1977.
Revised, updated and re-set and published in this edition in 1986.

© Sylvia Stanier, 1986

Published by J. A. Allen & Company Limited,
1, Lower Grosvenor Place, Buckingham Palace Road,
London, SW1W 0EL.

All rights reserved. No part of this book may be reproduced, stored in a retrieval system, or transmitted, in any form or by any means, electronic, mechanical, photocopying, recording or otherwise, without prior permission, in writing, from the publishers.

Book production Bill Ireson
Filmset by Fakenham Photosetting Limited, Fakenham, Norfolk
Printed by St. Edmundsbury Press, Bury St. Edmunds, Suffolk

Foreword

I knew Doreen Archer Houblon for many years and during her later years I was privileged to be closely associated with her and her side-saddle riding as well as having her as a guest in my house and being a guest in her most beautiful home in Kilkenny.

First and foremost Doreen was a true lady in the fullest meaning of that word – charming, humble, highly sophisticated and steeped in the arts, always impeccably turned out, appreciative of other people, highly knowledgeable in the fields of homoeopathy and organic farming, a lover of animals, a deep sense of devotion and loyalty to her Sovereign and great determination coupled with a willingness always to use her talents for the benefit of other people – humans and animals.

It was most rewarding to stay at Kilkenny amidst the innumerable treasures dating from King Charles II and Queen Anne, surrounded by an old time garden full of bees and butterflies, to see the devotion of her dogs and to gaze out into the park onto horses in the peak of condition and shining sleek cattle, a tribute to her total commitment to organic farming. To this must be added the esteem in which she was held in a part of the world which has not been spared its problems. Those are my memories of Doreen the lady.

Now to Doreen the side-saddle rider. I have been fortunate to be associated with side-saddles all my life – a method of riding so elegant and so well worth preserving, and having gone down so

FOREWORD

far, I am glad to see is rising again largely due to the Side-Saddle Association of which Doreen would so heartily approve.

Doreen's ability and determination came to the fore as soon as she sat in the saddle, especially on a difficult horse. She immediately but imperceptibly communicated to it what she wanted it to do, and that it was going to have to do it, so the sooner it relaxed and did it without fuss the better for both of them, and it almost invariably did. She was a most capable instructor, able to spot a problem, attributable to the fit of the saddle, the back, the withers or any other cause hidden to lesser experts, and she could tell a rider exactly which aid to apply in order to achieve the desired result, but, above all her talent and expertise were such that she could always do it better herself. I know of nobody who could produce a finished, comfortable, elegant, lady's side-saddle horse better than her.

It was Doreen's proudest achievement to have prepared The Queen's horse for Her Majesty's Birthday Parade for nineteen years and during that time she had to contend with some animals that were not exactly armchair rides. Over the years Doreen served Her Majesty to perfection and struck up a varied interest and friendship which lasted until the day she died.

I congratulate Sylvia Stanier and Mr Allen on reproducing this book, firstly because it is such an appropriate tribute to Doreen and secondly because it will be of inestimable value to aspiring side-saddle riders, and I commend it to a wide range of readers as being not only a technical classic but above all the story of a true and lovable lady.

John Miller

LT-COL SIR JOHN MILLER,
K.C.V.O., D.S.O., M.C.

*To Doreen Archer Houblon
and
"Joe" Hume Dudgeon
both of whom taught me so much*

Contents

	Page
FOREWORD *by Lt-Col Sir John Miller*, K.C.V.O., D.S.O., M.C.	v
LIST OF ILLUSTRATIONS	x
ACKNOWLEDGEMENTS	xii
INTRODUCTION	xiii
PART ONE: **Position**	1

Chapter
I	Broad Principles	3
II	Riding an Art of Movement	9

	Page
PART TWO: **Paces**	23
III Some notes on the horse's movement and the rider's reaction to these	25
PART THREE: **Aids**	31
IV Language of the Aids	33

CONTENTS

		Page
PART FOUR: ***Schooling***		43
V	Turns and Lateral Movements	45
VI	The Reins	49
VII	Cantering	54
PART FIVE: ***Jumping***		57
VIII	Movements of the Horse when Jumping	59

Appendices 69

I	Mounting and Dismounting	71
II	Fitting a Side-Saddle	74
III	Suppling Exercises	77

List of Illustrations

Frontispiece. Mrs Archer Houblon, C.V.O., riding "Imperial". From the painting by Terence Cuneo. Reproduced by Gracious Permission of H.M. The Queen

ILLUSTRATION PLATES

Plate		Between text pages
1	A suitable horse	10/11
2	Centralisation of weight	”
3	Normal seat in a side-saddle without a habit	”
4	Normal seat in a side-saddle with habit	”
5	Grip	”
6	Saddle fitting rider correctly	”
7	Riding a circle at walk	18/19
8	The trot	”
9	The canter (off-fore leading)	”
10	The canter (near-fore leading)	”
11	Opening gate	26/27
12	Going through gate	”
13	Shutting gate	”
14	Well turned out horse and rider	”
15	Well turned out horse and rider	”
16	Whip used as a substitute	34/35
17	Applying the leg	”
18	Correct position of hands at halt	”
19	Changing the reins into one hand	”
20	Changing the reins into one hand	”
21	Reins fully changed into one hand	”

LIST OF ILLUSTRATIONS

		Between text pages
22	Full pass to right at walk	34/35
23	Full pass to the left at walk	,,
24	Cavalletti at trot	66/67
25	A small fence	,,
26	Taking off (off-side)	,,
27	In the air (off-side)	,,
28	Landing (off-side)	,,
29	Take-off (near-side)	,,
30	In the air (near-side)	,,
31	Landing (near-side)	,,
32	Over the jump (near-side)	,,
33	Over the jump (off-side)	,,
34	A well balanced side-saddle	74/75
35	A well balanced side-saddle showing "Leaping Head" Pommel	,,
36	A stripped side-saddle (near-side)	,,
37	A stripped side-saddle (off-side)	,,
38	Stirrup bar, closed position (Mayhew)	,,
39	Stirrup bar, open position (Mayhew)	,,
40	Stirrup bar, closed with stirrup leather fitted (Mayhew)	,,
41	Stirrup iron and leather	,,
42	Girth for a side-saddle	,,

ILLUSTRATIONS IN THE TEXT

Figure	*Page*
The Opening Rein	50
The Indirect Rein (used behind the withers)	51

Acknowledgements

Original photographs by Major Archer Houblon. Other photographs supplied by Christina Belton, Charles Fennell, Monty, Tony Parkes.

The riders include Mrs Archer Houblon, Miss Elizabeth Sanford (Rosspir), Lady Stanier (Cufflink), Miss Sylvia Stanier (Bachelor Gay).

Consultancy Mrs W. Hanson.

I would particularly like to thank Mrs Caroline Burt for her tireless help and co-operation in the preparation of this book.

Introduction

Whilst I feel very privileged in helping to produce this edition of *Mrs Houblon's Side-Saddle*, I also feel a great responsibility. Mrs Archer Houblon's book *Side Saddle* was widely acknowledged as *the* manual on the subject of side-saddle riding, simply because it was based on the classical principles of horsemanship, which had been adapted and fitted into the sphere of side-saddle riding. In this new book I have tried to keep to as much of the original manuscript as possible.

Doreen Archer Houblon was not only a very fine horsewoman, she was a scholar of equitation, devoting much time and thought on how best to analyse and pass on her great knowledge. She took immense pleasure in doing so, and was one of the most precise and accurate people I have ever known, as well as being one of the kindest.

Although the book was first published in 1938 it had already taken several years of work to prepare it. Apart from her husband's great expertise with the camera, especially with the then rather new idea of cine camera, two other influences are also apparent. One was her friendship with the famous lady saddler, Miss Mayhew, secondly, the idea of the "Forward Seat" was just coming into vogue for jumping. Mrs Archer Houblon was quick to spot the great advantages of this position for side-saddle riders. So, with Miss Mayhew's design of a special "leaping head" pommel, Mrs Archer Houblon was able to

INTRODUCTION

advocate a radically altered position for a lady to adopt, over even the largest of fences, from that of being "left behind" to that of the now-a-days completely accepted "forward position".

Whilst some of the original photographs have been used for this edition, sadly some of the originals have become too faded to reproduce so a number of new photographs have been taken especially to illustrate Mrs Archer Houblon's principles as set out in the book. I would like to thank all those people who have helped in the production of these photographs, without their co-operation we should not have been able to produce this book.

Finally, I should like to quote a paragraph from Mrs Archer Houblon's own introduction to the 1950 Edition, which seems to me to be appropriate to this new 1986 book:

"In the text I have made a few necessary alterations, but here I should like to say how great a welcome should be extended and not least from the horse's point of view to the increased interest now being taken in dressage, not as some mystic word, but in its true meaning 'the correct fundamental training of the riding horse', whether he be hack or hunter, with its natural corollary 'the well trained rider'."

SYLVIA STANIER, L.V.O.
1986

Part One
Position

CHAPTER I

Broad Principles of Riding Astride and Side-Saddle. Advantages and Disadvantages of Riding Side-Saddle

The principles of riding and the ends at which we aim are exactly the same side-saddle as astride. This is a point that I should like to make clear from the beginning. Of course, there are certain details in execution which differ in the two modes of riding, and certain adaptations which have to be made when riding side-saddle; but the broad principles, the principles of balance, poise, suppleness, rhythm, sympathy, firmness of seat, independence of hands, and nicety in the application of the aids, remain the same, and so do the results which we strive to attain.

How, then, are we to decide whether to ride astride or side-saddle? I think the answer is that it depends on our physique. There are some women whose physique enables them to ride astride so beautifully that they do not feel it necessary to add riding side-saddle to their other accomplishments. Nevertheless, it is an undoubted fact that a side-saddle can give a woman a far firmer seat than she would ever have astride. Personal preference may well influence ladies today, in their efforts to revive the elegance and fashion of days gone by.

Strangely enough, it is this very firmness of seat which has brought the side-saddle into such disrepute. Some women, after a few rides, feel so secure that they do not realise that there is anything more to learn. They ride happily about the country on experienced and confidential horses, and are blissfully unaware of the discomfort they are causing them through the unbalanced distribution of their weight, and of the constant and anxious efforts of their grooms to keep their horses' backs from becoming sore. It never dawns on them that they are really little more than passengers, safely reaching their destinations only through the wisdom and tractability of their mounts. If anything goes wrong with their horses' backs it is always the fault of the saddle, never their own. If a horse goes badly with them it is his fault, never theirs! And they do not appreciate that further thought would disclose to them new possibilities in the way of sitting and riding their horses, which would make these troubles the exception rather than the rule. A great deal of help in the teaching and practice of side-saddle riding is being achieved through the Side-Saddle Equitation classes being held under the auspices of the Ladies' Side-Saddle Association at many leading horse shows.

The side-saddle has, for years and years, taken the blame for many things which were not its fault, though maybe they were not always the fault of the rider either, but of an incompetent saddler. The side-saddle is a difficult thing to make, its correct stuffing is no easy matter, and only the best saddlers can produce one that is really perfect. With a fundamentally unbalanced saddle what chance has even the most brilliant horsewoman of ever inducing it to keep straight on her horse's back?

So arose the ideas which so often make a woman hesitate to learn to ride side-saddle. She hears it said that in a side-saddle she will never be more than a passenger; that she will only be able to ride "made" horses; that she will not be able to ride awkward horses or "make" young ones; that she will have trouble in keeping her horses' backs right; that a side-saddle will only fit one or two horses for which it has been specially stuffed, and that it will rub every other horse.

She will find, however, that all these ideas are erroneous if she will learn and observe a few simple principles. She will find that her seat can be strong as well as firm; and by a strong seat I mean one that is balanced and supple, and yet so secure that it allows the rider to have hands that are completely independent of her seat and to use all the aids to their full advantage. Instead of being merely a passenger she can then be an "active" horsewoman, one who can, and does, freely use all the means at her disposal to make her horse submit to her wishes; and she will be able to ride awkward horses and make young ones. She will find that, in a good side-saddle with a general fitting tree, she will be able to ride any number of horses, ranging from, perhaps, 14·2 to 17 hands in height, without causing them discomfort. The side-saddle will not, of course, fit all these horses perfectly any more than would an astride saddle; but, if she sits in the right place, and in balance, she will be very unlikely to injure her horse's back. Thus one saddle will do for anything between a pony and a horse of average size.

If, however, she has also to ride many exceptionally wide horses, she would do well to have a second saddle with a broad-fitting tree, for such animals might stretch or even crack a general-fitting tree; but this is a point not peculiar to a side-saddle, for it applies equally to an astride saddle. There are some horses, of course, with abnormal backs, perhaps dipped, or thick and low in the withers, or with exceptionally high withers, and for these a side-saddle may have to be specially stuffed; but, again, for such horses similar adjustments would also be necessary with an ordinary astride saddle.

That horses have to be specially trained to carry a side-saddle is also a prevalent idea. It is thought that the rider's skirt will frighten them; that the balance strap will make them buck; that at first they will jump badly; and that a highly schooled horse will not be able to understand the indications of only the left leg, but will be, so to speak, searching for the support of the rider's right leg as well. When a horse encounters "drapery" for the first time he may quite possibly think it strange; but as this first encounter is usually with a rug worn at exercise, or a mackintosh worn by someone riding him astride, he has probably already got over his fear before meeting a skirt. If, however, he has had no such experience, a neat little skirt as worn today, would be a very good introduction. I have never known the balance strap make a horse buck; but in case I do ever meet the exception to the rule I make it a practice when mounting a horse that has never before carried a side-saddle, to wheel him sharply round several times both ways, in the smallest possible circle, to make sure that he has felt the balance strap. I have not yet known the side-saddle make the slightest difference to a horse jumping. Though at times it may appear to do so, the cause is the methods employed by that particular rider and not in the way that she is riding side-saddle. For a second or two, when first wanting to move forward in a side-saddle, the highly schooled horse will be puzzled by the absence of the rider's leg on his off-side. But as his first reaction to leg pressure without restraint from there should be to advance, he will do so, and the doubt will quickly fade. Years ago there was a famous character who hunted in Ireland who habitually wore only one spur. When asked the reason why he answered: "Ach, shure where one side of a horse goes the other side has got to go too!" Every indication of leg and hand means on a side-saddle, exactly what it means when applied by a person riding astride; but the point is that to obtain certain results when riding side-saddle they are applied in different combinations. If the horse obeys each indication implicitly the desired result is obtained and the more highly a horse is schooled, the more perfectly he will understand the clearly expressed wishes of his rider.

Thus the major arguments against the side-saddle are seen to be without foundation when it is understood that they are bad instances of its misuse.

Let us now turn to minor considerations.

The side-saddle is, in itself, a little heavier than an astride saddle, an average side-saddle weighing about 20 lb (9 kg) and an astride about 11 lb (5 kg), but this additional weight makes little difference when the horse is already hardly up to the weight of the rider.

It is also argued that a woman rides heavier in a side-saddle due to her weight not being placed over the horse's centre of gravity, but this need not be so, as we shall see later. When buying a side-saddle it is important that it should have the modern, straight seat and not the old-fashioned, dipped seat in which it is so difficult to keep one's weight correctly placed.

As newly made side-saddles are both rare and extremely expensive, most sales are of "secondhand" saddles, or pre-war trees with new leather work and stuffing. These saddles usually bear famous names such as Mayhew, Owen, Champion and Wilton etc.

That a woman is less independent in a side-saddle, it being difficult for her to get on and off, open gates, etc., is without any foundation whatsoever.

That side-saddle habits are more expensive than clothes for riding astride is, in a sense, true because of the addition of the skirt. Custom still dictates that this should be worn for hunting and showing, and what a comfort it is over our knees on a cold, wet day! But for ordinary hacking in the country what need is there to cover with a skirt a well-cut pair of Jodhpurs or boots and breeches, on a figure that would go about skirtless quite happily were she riding astride?

The question of the comparative degree of danger in riding side-saddle or astride is, I think, difficult to decide. The firmer seat in a side-saddle undoubtedly saves many a fall; the rider will be much less likely to be bucked or jumped off than she would be astride, and she will find it much easier to sit quietly and give her horse complete freedom of head to recover if he gets into difficulties over a fence. On the other hand, if a horse really does fall and roll over it is more difficult for her to get clear of him than it would be were she riding astride. So we have to try and weigh up the many falls that are avoided when riding side-saddle against the possibility of more serious consequences if a fall should occur.

It adds to the comfort and safety of riding if the saddle, especially as regards the size, shape, and setting of the pommels, fits the rider. This means that she will often prefer to take her own saddle about with her, a trouble she would not have were she riding astride. Nowadays many astride riders do indeed take their own saddles about with them.

Though some women never seem to feel it I think it is true that riding side-saddle is more tiring to many than riding astride. Instead of the work being done equally by both sides of the body, this in part, in a side-saddle, is done by the right leg and thigh. Usually the beginner starts with only a short ride every day she may then become tired, and disheartened, and she may imagine that she will then be uncomfortable. But let her rest assured that this is not so, she will need time and patience, but if she takes the trouble to develop a good seat she will find it comfortable as well as strong.

From all this it will be seen that there are a few small disadvantages in riding side-saddle, but surely these are completely outweighed by the enormous advantages of the added security and strength it gives.

CHAPTER II

Riding an Art of Movement. Balanced Seat Aimed At. Grip. Details of "Key Position" of Seat and Hands

Let us get deeply into our consciousness the idea that riding is an art of movement as well as one of horse psychology. There should be no involuntary fixity or stiffness anywhere, either in our bodies or in our minds. Our horse is a living being and, though in a sense we control his movements, yet the movements are his. Every horse gives us a different "feel", and it is this "feel", this movement, with which we want to be in harmony. Unless we are in harmony we do not get the true "feel", and it is only through close touch with our horse and a sense of balance, rhythm, and sympathy that this harmony can be attained. So we want to adopt a position in the saddle which enables us most easily to achieve this end.

Going into more detail, we aim at a seat which, as well as being balanced, is comfortable, strong, and secure. It should counteract, as far as possible, the unequal distribution of the rider's weight caused by both her legs being on the same side of her horse; it should help her to keep her weight, with little muscular effort, in a place comfortable for herself and for him; and it should give her security and yet allow her to use her muscles and joints with freedom and suppleness when necessary.

Balance, then, is one of the first essentials of riding, but circumstances will sometimes arise when the rider, through some quick or unexpected movement of her horse, will lose her balance unless to retain her position she can bring grip speedily to her aid.

Grip in a side-saddle is not, as is sometimes supposed, a kind of pincer action of the thighs down against the top pommel and up against the lower one. It is something quite different. The rider gets a "purchase" (it cannot exactly be called a "grip") with the right leg by pressing the outside of the leg right down to the ankle, against the flap of the saddle where it lies against the horse's shoulder; at the same time pressing the inside of the right thigh to the left against the top pommel. This double purchase, in combination with the support of the left thigh against the saddle, is the normal means by which a rider retains her position when her balance is threatened. In addition she can bring a "reserve grip" into play by pressing the left thigh forward, or, in certain cases, up, against the leaping head as well as in against the saddle. In this "reserve grip" lies the greater firmness of seat given by the side-saddle as opposed to an astride saddle. For example, if we are bucked or jumped off it is nearly always due to our being caught unawares or out of timing and being displaced by the upward punch of the horse's spring. In a side-saddle we have the leaping head against which we press our thigh and which we use as a "stop" to prevent our body from being punched up and perhaps forward off the saddle. Nevertheless, we must not use our "reserve grip" continuously, for, though it might add to our security, it would deprive us of much of the freedom of movement which is essential to us if we are to be strong horsewomen.

In developing a seat there are seven points to which the beginner should pay great attention until she has not only acquired a good position but can maintain it subconsciously.

1. The first, and perhaps the most important of all, is that the

Plate 1 A SUITABLE HORSE
A High Class Ladies "Leicestershire" Hunter, well balanced, showing substance and quality, plus a correctly made back and withers to carry a side-saddle easily.

Plate 2 CENTRALISATION OF WEIGHT
The Rider should feel that the major part of her weight is gathered together over the spot where her right thigh crosses the horse's backbone.

Plate 3 NORMAL SEAT IN A SIDE-SADDLE
Without a habit.

Plate 4 NORMAL SEAT IN A SIDE-SADDLE
With a habit correctly fitted.

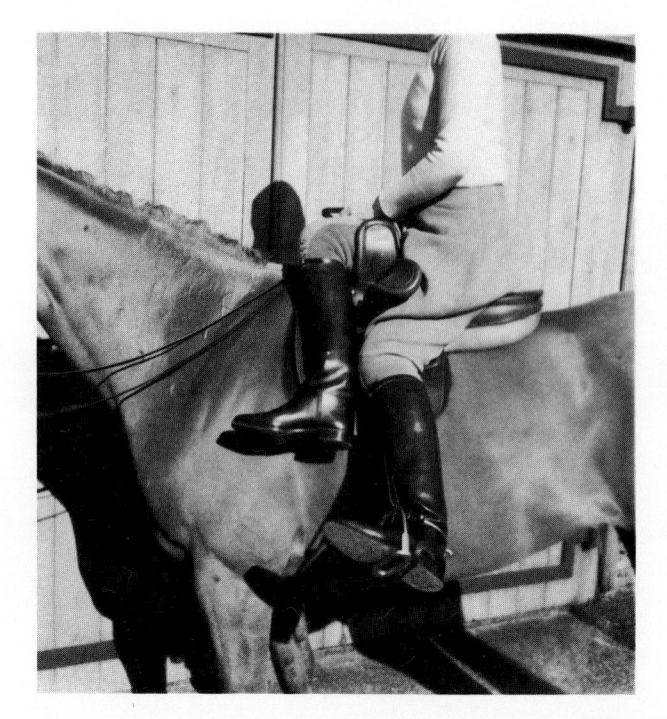

Plate 5 GRIP
Correct position of legs, using normal grip, in combination with support of left thigh and knee against saddle and right outside calf muscles against saddle, plus right heel back towards left shin.

Plate 6 SADDLE FITTING RIDER CORRECTLY
Normal clearance between angle of right knee and front of top pommel. Thickness of hand between leaping head and thigh.

base of the rider's spine should at all times be directly over the horse's backbone, and except in special circumstances, the line of the spine as a whole should also be in the same vertical plane as that of her horse. For instance, when swinging the body forward in rhythm with him the rider should go forward so straight that a plumb line dropped through any part of her spine would pass through a part of his spine immediately below it.

Of course, there are times when she may purposely incline her body a little to one side or the other, but, even then, the base of her spine should keep to its central position like the roots of a tree as it sways in the wind.

2. Her hips should be as square to the front as her build will allow.
3. Her shoulders should be square to the front and level.
4. The right thigh (*i.e.*, from seatbone to knee), on which, as we shall see later, nearly the whole of the rider's weight is borne, lies along the top of the saddle, and should cross the horse's backbone just behind the withers, the point at which it is most comfortable for him to carry weight. From the knee downwards, her right leg should hang perpendicularly or even a little behind the perpendicular, lying against the flap of the saddle.
5. Her left thigh should lie on the saddle, roughly at an angle of 45 degrees, and the lower part of the leg, from the knee downwards, should hang just behind the perpendicular.
6. Her weight should be borne on her right thigh in such a way that, though it is actually distributed all along her thigh from the seatbone forward, yet she *feels* that the major part is gathered together over the spot where her thigh crosses her horse's backbone. She should draw the weight off her left seatbone forward and to the right until she has the impression that her centre of gravity is over the desired spot. This point, though differing from the teaching of some authorities, is, in my opinion, of vital importance. In

movement, of course, the weight does not remain always over this central spot; but will be borne at different points along the right thigh, from the seatbone, when, for instance, driving a horse on, to only just behind the knee when in the most forward position over a big fence.
7. The rider should sit erect, poised and supple, with her back held naturally.

These, in brief, are the guiding principles of the side-saddle seat. Let us consider them more in detail.

Nearly every beginner seems to realise instinctively the need for a more equal distribution of her weight than is produced by sitting evenly on both seatbones when, in a side-saddle, the weight of the whole of one leg and a great part of the other are on one side of her horse.

I suggest that the solution of the problem of centralising the weight is to be found in points (1), (2), and (6) above:

1. Keeping the base of the spine over the horse's backbone and the spine as a whole in the same vertical plane as that of the horse.
2. Keeping the hips as square to the front as the build of the rider will allow.
6. Placing the weight on the right thigh and endeavouring to poise it so that, though it is actually distributed all along her thigh from the seatbone forward, yet she *feels* that the major part is gathered together over the spot where her thigh crosses the horse's backbone.

Sitting with equal weight on both seatbones the rider will find that her left hip is further back than her right, and that, as we have already seen, she has an excessive proportion of her total weight on the near side of her horse. By bringing her left hip forward she will automatically take weight off her left seatbone, and, by drawing that weight forward and to the right, she will *feel* that her centre of gravity is over the spot where her right thigh (from seatbone to knee) crosses her horse's backbone. To attain this position she should on no account hollow her back, neither should she move *bodily* forward in the saddle, but merely move her left hip forward and transfer her *weight*, poising it in a central position over her horse. (The beginner will find it helpful to imagine that there is a tintack sticking up on the left side of the seat of her saddle, and that she must avoid sitting down on it!) She will then find that she can adjust her balance to the movement of her horse more easily; her weight will be in a good position for him to carry it; she will no longer feel that her saddle has any tendency to pull over to the left; and it will sit comfortably on many horses of varying conformation.

Some beginners try to adjust the distribution of their weight by leaning out to the right, so that a plumb line dropped from the back of their neck would fall well to the off side of their horse. This does have the effect of putting the weight on the right thigh, but besides being a tiring posture to maintain, it is not well balanced and takes away from both the security and strength of the seat. The normal position in the saddle should be the one which allows the greatest freedom of movement to the body, and this condition cannot be fulfilled if the rider is already leaning out to the right. It should also be in a direct line between the source of impulsion (*i.e.*, his loins and quarters) and the point at which that impulsion is controlled (*i.e.*, the mouth). If she is leaning out to the right she is not in that strong position, and she is also deprived of the support of her left thigh against the saddle.

Other riders, having tried leaning out to the right and realising that they are not sitting straight, and that their left shoulder is higher than their right, endeavour to improve matters by bringing just their neck or the upper vertebrae of their spine into the right vertical plane and dropping their left shoulder. But this only results in a curved spine, a cramped seat, and the weight still in the wrong place.

The habit of sitting with the base of the spine on the near side of the saddle makes matters still worse. It is often due to there being too much room where the thigh fits into the top pommel. This lets the rider slip down on to the near side of her saddle, and makes it very difficult for her to sit in the middle of the seat. A saddler can easily rectify this by putting more stuffing on the pommel.

Some riders go to the opposite extreme in their efforts to adjust their weight and sit too far over on the off side. This not only forces the right hip forward and tends to put the rider out of balance, but it prevents the full use of the left thigh, and is an insecure position.

This brings us back to the question of keeping the hips as square to the front as the build of the rider will allow, a precept which is easier to obey for a woman of slim figure, long from hip to knee, than it is for one less favoured by nature. It will be found that the tendency in a side-saddle is for the right hip to be further forward than the left; but the drawing of the weight off the left seatbone forward and to the right will help very much in bringing the left hip forward into a square position. Likewise, putting the hip in the right position helps in the adjustment of the weight and in keeping the left knee and thigh on the saddle.

Now let us pass on to the remaining points:

3. The shoulders should be absolutely square to the front and level.

The general tendency is for the right shoulder to go forward. This eventually brings too much of the rider's weight over to the off side and puts her out of balance. She is then no longer in a position to press her thigh firmly under the leaping head, it will merely rotate round it, and her "reserve grip", which she so much needs to help her to regain her balance, is lost.

Beginners lose their balance and fall off in this way very easily, and even a rider with a certain amount of experience may find it hard not to do so if her horse whips round very sharply to the left, or bucks rapidly in that direction.

So important is it not to let the right shoulder come further forward than the left that this tendency should be deliberately anticipated, and, if possible, prevented, should anything arise which is likely to put our security to the test.

Beginners find it very difficult to prevent this displacement when going in a left-handed circle, or when riding a horse that is not easy for them to steady, or that makes any abnormal movement such as even a "pig jump". (A species of half buck.) So disastrous are its results that the necessity for guarding against it cannot be too strongly emphasised.

An exercise that helps to instil the right counteracting movement into the mind of the beginner is to place her in a good position, tell her to keep absolutely still from the waist downwards, and then make her turn to the right from just above the waist, forcing her right shoulder and side round and as far back as they will go, and at the same time letting her left shoulder come as far forward as her right shoulder has gone back. But on no account should the shoulders be humped or rounded, and the head should be held erect.

As regards keeping the shoulders level, there are some people who naturally carry one shoulder higher than the other, and who will continue to do so when riding; but a droop of either shoulder in the case of a normal person produces a curve of the spine to the detriment of the seat.

Some beginners, when asked to put their right shoulder back, will also drop it, but this should not be allowed.

Because the tendency is for the right shoulder to go forward the idea which the beginner should instil into her mind is to keep it back; but it is sometimes helpful, when trying to acquire a straight and easy seat, to think of keeping the *left* shoulder and hip forward, by this means keeping the hips and shoulders square to the front, and counteracting the tendency of some beginners to lean the whole body too far back.

4. The right thigh, bearing nearly the whole of the rider's weight, lies along the top of the saddle, and should cross the horse's backbone just behind the withers; and the right leg, from the knee downwards, should hang perpendicularly or even a little behind the perpendicular, lying against the flap of the saddle.

At moments when the strongest grip is being exerted, it may be found helpful in some saddles to draw the right heel back, so that it touches the shin of the left leg.

As has already been described when discussing grip, the function of the right leg is to assist in the retention of balance by pressing the outside of the leg and ankle against the flap of the saddle and the inside of the thigh against the top pommel. Beginners as a rule do not make enough use of this "purchase"; in fact they often seriously weaken the support which can be derived from it by twisting the foot and ankle away from the saddle. The further down the leg the rider can apply the pressure, even right down to and including the foot, the stronger and more useful to her will be this purchase.

The right leg should not be allowed to poke forward, as this reduces the amount of pressure that can be exerted, places the weight of the body too far back and impairs the suppleness of the seat. If, in this position, the rider attempts to bend her body forward from the hips, she will find the movement restrained by the muscles of her right thigh where it lies on the saddle; whereas she will find no difficulty in the movement if she keeps her leg hanging perpendicularly. With her leg poked forward she will also find it impossible to avoid sitting with her weight too far back. Sore backs often result from this faulty position, which brings too much bearing on the edge of the pannels, causing them to "scald" the back, and, unless the saddle fits the horse perfectly, it will be dragged over to the left and may bruise the off side of the withers.

There should be a certain clearance between the inside angle of the right knee and the front of the top pommel. Its extent will depend largely on the build of the saddle and the width of the pommel, but it should not be less than half an inch (1·25 cm). On the other hand, it should not be too great. Some people are over-anxious not to sit too far back, and go to the other extreme of sitting too far forward. In this position they have little or no control over a difficult horse, and their weight is placed too much on the horse's forehand.

5. The left thigh should lie on the saddle, roughly at an angle of 45 degrees; and the lower part of the leg, from the knee downwards, should hang just behind the perpendicular.

By thigh I mean the whole of the limb down to the knee. It has three functions:

1. To be ready to assist in the retention of balance, which means that it must never be allowed to lose contact with the saddle.
2. To bring into play the "reserve grip" already mentioned, by pressing against the leaping head as well as in against the saddle.
3. To act as a "prop" to assist in preventing the weight being pulled or thrown too far forward. In this capacity its action is specially useful when riding a pulling horse.

The slope of the thigh is affected by the length of the stirrup leather. If the leather is too short it raises the knee too high, thus cramping the seat, throwing the weight of the body too far back and restricting the use of the leg for the application of the aids. If, on the other hand, the leather is too long, the thigh will hang too steeply and it will be deprived of much of its power as a "prop". The rider will also have a tendency to slip down on the near side of her saddle, and it will sorely tax the muscles of her right thigh to resist this tendency.

In a saddle that fits the rider there should be about the thickness of a hand between the thigh and the leaping head, but it is the slope at which the thigh should rest, and not the position of the leaping head in regard to the thigh, which regulates the length of the stirrup leather. If a saddle does not fit the rider, and the leaping head is placed too high, it will obviously only cramp the seat and throw the weight too far back if the stirrup leather is taken up until there is only room for the thickness of a hand between the thigh and the leaping head. In such a saddle the rider should keep her stirrup leather at the length which allows her thigh to be at the proper angle even though she may lose her iron should she have to call her reserve grip into play.

If the leaping head is set too low it may necessitate the rider having her thigh constantly pressed against it, or it may even force her thigh too far back. The first position makes her feel cramped and uncomfortable, and as if she were wedged between stirrup and leaping head; and the second makes her seat extremely insecure. It is better not to ride in a saddle with the leaping head set thus if it can possibly be avoided; on the other hand, once a rider is accustomed to a leaping head which is set too high, she will neither feel so uncomfortable nor so insecure as might be imagined.

Some people maintain that the thigh should never have to be moved upwards to meet the leaping head, but how can this be right? If it is set so as to touch the thigh continuously, the rider's leg is wedged between it and the stirrup, which is a cramped position and surely must be dangerous. There ought, therefore, to be a space between the two; and if the leaping head is to be brought into use this space can only be bridged by movement. In many cases a slipping forward and a rolling inwards of the left thigh will suffice; but where we are caught napping with our weight back and where a definite grip is needed to prevent our being "punched" upwards or losing our balance to the right, an upward movement of the thigh is necessary. This, of course, may take the weight of the foot off the stirrup, but, with the heel

Plate 7 RIDING A CIRCLE AT WALK
The horse glancing in the direction in which he is moving, the rider is also looking in the same direction.

Plate 8 THE TROT
A well balanced trot, with the rider sitting easily and in balance with the horse's movement.

Plate 9 THE CANTER (off-fore leading)
The horse is going forwards and the rider is sitting in balance (compare with No. 10 for different adjustment of balance).

Plate 10 THE CANTER (near-fore leading)
The horse is in a different part of the canter stride and the rider has adjusted her position accordingly.

well down, it will seldom be lost. If the iron does leave the foot it does not really matter, for the stirrup should only be used to help in supporting the weight of the leg. None of the weight of the body should ever rest on it, and the seat should in no way be impaired by its loss.

Though the left thigh and knee should not be actively *pressed* against the saddle except when it is necessary to exert grip, they should rest in continuous contact with it so that the thigh may be ready instantly to fulfil its first function of assisting in the retention of balance, and also to ensure that when it is called upon to use the "reserve grip" its natural direction of movement is not outwards but inwards towards the angle of pommel and saddle. Many a rider, when hoping to use this grip, has become "unhooked" through bringing her thigh up and out, thus missing her pommel and finding her thigh above it! She may then have a fall which could have been avoided had the thigh been kept habitually on the saddle. This contact, as I have said before, is achieved, not so much by actually pressing the thigh inwards, as by keeping the left hip forward and in line with the right hip, when it will be found that the left thigh lies naturally on the saddle and is automatically kept in proper contact with it. If, however, the rider allows her left hip to go back and her weight to come down on to her left seatbone, her knee will fall away from the saddle unless consciously pressed against it.

The knee should be perfectly supple, otherwise the leg from the knee downwards loses much of its efficiency in applying the aids.

The lower part of the leg, below the knee, should hang "just behind the perpendicular". This is a vague term, and perhaps it would be a better guide to say that the leg will be in the right position when, with the stirrup leather at the correct length, the foot placed "home" in the iron, the knee in front of the leather and the ankle behind it, the stirrup leather is hanging perpendicular.

If the left leg is allowed to poke forward it has the effect, as in the case of the right leg, of throwing the weight too far back and impairing the rider's suppleness; and it may also indicate a stiff knee.

If the left leg is allowed to go too far back the sympathetic application of the aids will be well-nigh impossible. It is a position which, especially at the canter or the gallop, often results in the leg being pressed into the horse's side, confusing a well-schooled animal and possibly goading him into an uncomfortable state of agitation. The faster the horse wants to go the more the rider presses her leg into his side, and the harder she does so the more he is urged to increase his speed – a vicious circle!

No attempt should be made to turn the toe either inwards or outwards. It should point in the direction natural to the rider. If the toe is forced out it tends to turn the knee out also, and in extreme cases causes it to leave the saddle altogether. If it is turned too far inwards it makes it impossible to use the leg to its full advantage.

The heel should be down. This braces the muscles of the calf, making the leg far more effective for the application of the aids. It also helps the thigh to lie comfortably on the saddle. A slight bend at the ankle and an increased pressure of the inside edge of the sole of the boot against the stirrup iron, making the sole face slightly away from the horse, will help to ensure that the knee is close into the saddle and reduce the risk of the rider becoming "unhooked" or unbalanced. When trying to put the foot in this position great care should be taken not to alter the direction in which the toe is pointing, but to keep it in its natural position. It will be found that a contrary bend at the ankle to that just described will encourage the knee to move away from the saddle – a thing to be avoided.

The stirrup should only be used as a support for some of the weight of the leg. Little of the weight of the thigh and none of the weight of the body should ever be allowed to come down on to it. Consequently the pressure on it should only be very slight.

For this reason, when not having the smoothest of rides either owing to the horse or the country or both, the rider is far less likely to lose her iron if she rides with it "home" rather than on the ball of the foot. The latter may be better for high school riding, but the former is undoubtedly more practical for everyday work.

7. The rider should sit erect, poised and supple, with her back held naturally.

She should on no account hollow her back, as this automatically creates stiffness and prevents the loins moving freely in touch with the movements of her horse, a matter of vital importance, as we shall see in the next chapter.

The upper part of the arm should be allowed to hang loosely and naturally, close to the sides, with the forearm held more or less horizontally, and the hands almost meeting in front of the centre of the body.

The wrists should be rounded, with the backs of the hands facing half-right and half-left as the case may be. The line of the knuckles should be perpendicular, the thumbs on top, and the hands neither higher nor lower than the wrists. Care should be taken that this position of the hands is attained by rounding the wrists, and not by sticking out the elbows. It should be clearly understood, however, that the hands should not be held rigidly in this manner; but that it is the "key position" from which the fingers and wrists can obtain a great degree of suppleness and respond sympathetically to the movements of the horse.

The hands, to be active and sympathetic, should be held just clear of the lap. If they are allowed to rest on it they are, for the time being, dead and inactive or definitely an interference to the movements of the horse. For show riding some women keep their hands as low as possible, the right hand almost touching the flap of the saddle below the right thigh and the left hand equally low on the near side; but this is done with the idea of improving the look of the horse's forehand in the eyes of the judges and does not apply to ordinary riding.

What a heavy chapter this has been! But I think this is unavoidable. It is like laying the foundation of a building. The lower stones must be big and solid. The foundation must be well and truly laid.

Let it be fully realised that we have only been describing the *key* position to a good seat, not a position to be rigidly adhered to. It is the position from which, I think, a rider can most freely move every joint and muscle, and can most easily move her weight according to the needs of the moment and ride in balance and poise. There is such a vast difference between the woman who sits stiffly in a "good position" on *top* of her horse, and the woman who sits *into* her horse and who is so much one with him that they seem to merge into one another, and move together like the waters of a river flowing down to the sea.

Part Two
Paces

CHAPTER III

Some notes on the horse's movement and the rider's reaction to these

When riding either astride or side-saddle it is important for the rider to have supple use of her loins, enabling the upper part of the body to travel smoothly and steadily, like the chassis of a well-sprung car!

The rider's adjustment of the position of her centre of gravity to become in harmony with her horse is of paramount importance. At slow paces the forward inclination of the body is but slight; at fast paces it must be greater; until, when jumping one should lean right forward, not only to enable the adjustments to keep pace with the rapidity of the horse's movements, but also to be in a position of balance, particularly when the horse's body is nearing the vertical position at the point of take-off at a jump. She must, however, always try to move *with* her horse – never a fraction of a second before him, or after him.

Let us now consider the horse's paces, and see how a side-saddle rider should react to them.

Walking

The walk is a pace of four time, each foot coming to the ground in turn. At the walk the adjustment of the rider's weight is so slight as to be almost imperceptible; but her loins will be rounding and straightening in response to the forward movement of her horse.

Trotting

The trot is a two-time movement; the near-fore and the off-hind (left diagonal) coming down together, by the off-fore and near-hind (right diagonal) also coming down together.

Some horses, at a slow trot, are so smooth that they hardly move a supple rider, and it is not necessary to "rise". To "rise" means that the rider sits down in the saddle when one diagonal is on the ground and rises when the other is coming down. The rider is said to be "riding on the right diagonal" when she is sitting down on it and rising with the left diagonal and *vice versa*. It is therefore a good idea for a rider to study the horses paces – particularly the trot, for in side-saddle riding the trot is one of the most difficult paces at which to keep one's balance.

To "rise" at the trot the rider should lean her body slightly forward, and think of rising *forward* rather than up. She should rise as short a distance out of the saddle as the horses stride will allow.

It cannot be repeated too often that the "rise" should come from the movement of the horse, assisted by the right thigh, and *not* from the stirrup; and that great care should be taken to see that the rider's spine remains central to that of the horse.

If you ride along behind a lady riding side-saddle, who is rising correctly, you will notice that her saddle has very little movement, simply that which is caused by the movement of the horse's hindquarters. Someone rising incorrectly will move the saddle very considerably from side to side (usually by rising from pressing off the stirrup instead of the thigh). This movement of the saddle is one of the major causes of horse's backs becoming sore and bruised when ridden side-saddle.

It is often a good idea to change from riding on one particular

Plate 11 OPENING GATE
The horse is correctly placed to allow rider to open the gate.

Plate 12 GOING THROUGH THE GATE
The rider pushing the gate open with her right hand.

Plate 13 SHUTTING THE GATE
The rider using her right hand on the gate, will indicate to the horse to move to the right with her left leg.

Plates 14 (above) and 15 (below) GOOD TURNOUT *Well fitting saddlery and both riders well turned out.*

diagonal to riding on the opposite one. This will ease the burden to the horse's back and to his legs. How, one may ask, does the rider achieve this change of diagonal? She does this by sitting down for two strides instead of one; this may give a kind of "bumping" feeling, until one becomes used to doing this change over. It will be a temptation to sit for three strides, until one gets the timing correct. It is often a help to say to oneself "down, up, down, up", to achieve a rhythm, and then it is easy to say "down, up, down, up".

The sequence to be followed for the change of diagonal by the rider is:

Left diagonal	SIT	Right diagonal	RISE
,, ,,	SIT	,, ,,	RISE
,, ,,	SIT	,, ,,	SIT
,, ,,	RISE	,, ,,	SIT

It is best to achieve a nice rhythmical trot on one diagonal before attempting to change diagonals.

Cantering

The canter is a pace of three-time. A horse is said to "lead" with the foreleg which is extended furthest to the front. The order in which the horse's legs take the weight of his body if the off-foreleg is "leading", is: (1) near hind; (2) off-hind and near fore together; (3) off-fore. Broadly speaking, it feels to the rider as though the horse were taking a series of smooth leaps.

The rider, to keep in balance, must allow her loins to react in a supple manner in exact liaison with the horse's stride, so that whilst her upper body may move a little her seat remains comfortably in contact with the saddle. If the rider stiffens her body she will be bumped into the air at each stride – both uncomfortable for the rider and damaging to the horse's back.

Most riders today learn to ride in an enclosed arena, so

circling at any pace comes early in the programme. Thus it is important and relevant to study this movement. When cantering on a circle the rider should incline her body slightly inwards, the amount depending on the speed of the horse and the size of the circle. It is usually best to commence canter circle work on a circle of not less than approximately 27 yds (25 m). Incidentally, the left rein is the more difficult of the two reins on which to canter. I would therefore advocate teaching canter in side-saddle on the right rein.

Because of the fact that the major part of the side-saddle, plus the rider, is situated on the near or left side of the horse, it follows that there can be some restriction of the horse's left shoulder and thus reluctance on the part of the horse to canter freely on this rein if he, and his rider, are not used to doing so. The tendency with the beginner rider is to find her right shoulder moving forwards, thus forcing her to relax the pressure of her right leg and left thigh against the saddle, effecting a loss of balance. To counteract this problem the rider must concentrate on keeping her right shoulder in place and try to feel her balance is correct, by using, really strongly, the purchase obtained by pressing the lower part of her right leg against the top pommel, and her left thigh hard against the saddle, *but* without raising it upwards into the leaping head. Gradually the rider will learn to keep her body in balance without having to use any extra grip.

The same advice applies to riding a horse which pulls. It will be seen, therefore, that concentration on keeping the right shoulder in place is of the utmost importance.

Galloping

The gallop, being a very fast pace and therefore not as controllable as the canter, is not recommended for the beginner.

It is a pace of four-time with a moment of "suspension" when all four of the horse's legs are off the ground together, just prior to the next sequence commencing.

SOME NOTES ON THE HORSE'S MOVEMENT

When galloping – which is a pace required in the show ring and often in the hunting field – our purpose is to assist the horse to move freely. With this in view, the rider should have her weight well forward, with less burden on the horse's back and quarter muscles. The rider's weight should be "cushioned" on her thighs rather than on the saddle – occasionally it may be a good idea to actually take one's seat bones off the saddle. Some riders like also to make a "bridge" with the reins across the horse's neck on which to lean. This is a matter of personal preference, and it should be stated that (1) contact with the reins to the horse's mouth should be maintained at all times in the gallop; and (2) it is not a good idea to "lean" on the reins in such a way as to be continually pulling backwards on them.

The aim of a good position at the gallop is to sail along smoothly without bumping up and down on the saddle.

Part Three
Aids

CHAPTER IV

ABC of Language of the Aids. The Leg. Stiffness, its Cause and Effect. Weight of the Body. Hands. Method of Holding Reins. Methods of Guiding. Keeping a Smooth Feel on Horse's Mouth. "Hands." Voice. Whip. Spur

This chapter deals largely with first principles and is written with the idea of helping beginners; so the more experienced horsewoman must skim over the elementary paragraphs until she finds something which attracts her attention.

When riding we tell our horse what to do by means of the leg, the weight of the body, the hands through the medium of the reins, and the voice. These, in equitation, are called the "natural aids". Through them we should express our wishes sympathetically and clearly. As long as a horse understands our indications he is, as a rule, only too anxious to obey; but if the aids are applied unsympathetically or with uncertainty, or if we contradict them by unintentionally applying some other aid at the same time, he may instead be frightened, fussed, or puzzled.

It is well, therefore, to learn the ABC of the language of the aids before attempting to use the large vocabulary of the skilled horsewoman; and so in this chapter we will discuss the leg, only as used to ask our horse to move forward; and the hands, only as regards the way in which they hold the reins and are used for stopping and guiding him.

The Leg

Pressure of the leg on the horse's side tells him to move forward. The area just behind the girth will be found to produce the most response to this leg pressure owing to the sensory nerves running near the surface at this spot. If a steady pressure does not produce the desired result, intermittent pressure may be tried and, should this fail, then the leg may be applied to the horse's side in a series of taps, which in extreme cases can almost amount to blows.

There is a widespread but erroneous idea that it is the heel which should be used to give the indication to move. In actual fact it is the pressure of the calf of the leg, sometimes assisted by the heel. In applying the pressure of the leg, the knee and thigh should not move from their normal place on the saddle; but, with an absolutely supple knee joint, the leg, from the knee downwards, should be moved from its normal position backwards and inwards so that the inside of the back of the calf meets the horse's side. The side-saddle rider's left leg, especially the part below the knee, should work in a similar manner as when riding astride.

Many riders are so stiff that they find great difficulty in using their legs effectively. Every muscle has its counterpart. For instance, the leg has certain muscles which bend the knee and draw the lower part of the leg back. Their counterparts draw the leg forward and straighten the knee. The stiff woman cannot help bringing into play, not only those muscles which are necessary to draw the leg back, but also their counterparts. This produces rigidity and immobility of the limb. She works so hard that she soon becomes tired, but in spite of all her efforts attains no result. Her muscles are only working against each other, mutually preventing any free movement; and the horse remains

Plate 16 WHIP USED AS A SUBSTITUTE
Rider's leg on off-side. A long whip is being used to allow rider to use the reins with both hands.

Plate 17 APPLYING THE LEG
Inside of back of calf of rider's left leg is pressed against the horse's side.

Plate 18 CORRECT POSIT-
ION OF HANDS AT HALT
The reins held in two hands.

Plate 19 CHANGING THE REINS INTO ONE
HAND (Left)
*Showing first adjustment – slipping right hand back
along the reins.*

Plate 20 CHANGING THE REINS INTO ONE HAND
Next part of the adjustment, placing right reins into left hand at the spot at which they were held by the right hand.

Plate 21 REINS IN ONE HAND
Reins now neatly all held by the left hand.

Plate 22 FULL PASS TO RIGHT AT WALK
Note position of horse throughout, also application of rider's left leg.

Plate 23 FULL PASS TO THE LEFT
Here the rider is substituting her right leg with a short whip. All reins are in one hand, but the wrist is used so that the horse's head is bent at the poll in the direction in which he is moving.

totally unaware that a severe application of the leg was even intended!

The supple woman uses only the muscles which draw backwards the part of the leg below the knee; so that the movement is free, and, should she so desire it, the force with which the leg comes into her horse's side has in it almost a sting.

The rider's leg should not be moved forward before being pressed back on to the horse's side. It should merely move from its normal position backwards and inwards. The muscles should then be relaxed and the leg will return to its natural position.

The leg should not be "flapped" against the horse's side with a movement working on a line at right angles to his body, when only the inside of the calf and ankle will come in contact with him. This is bound to be a stiff and weak movement owing to the fact that the knee joint is designed to allow the lower leg to bend backwards and forwards, rather than from side to side. The movement should be backwards and inwards, bringing the inner part of the back of the calf (*i.e.*, from the back seam of the boot round the inside) against the horse.

The knee and thigh should not be allowed to leave the saddle, for, should her horse make a sudden movement, the rider would then be in danger of becoming unbalanced. The lower part of the leg must, therefore, be moved independently of the thigh, and to make this possible, the knee joint must be supple.

The toe must not be allowed to go down and the heel up, as this makes the calf of the leg soft, flabby, and ineffective in its pressure on the horse's side; the muscles of the thigh are also affected and its efficiency is considerably impaired.

The beginner will find that, if she has to use her leg strongly, it is hard to avoid letting other parts of her body, especially her arms and hands, move in time with her leg. She should be on her guard against this, and do all in her power to prevent such movement. Her leg should drive her horse on, not into hands which are jerking involuntarily, but into hands which are controlled and quiet.

All the aids must be applied smoothly, and with only sufficient force to command obedience. The leg should never be applied more severely than is necessary, and, when riding a strange horse, the rider will do well to feel her way with him until she finds out whether or not he is sensitive to the leg. Horses vary in this respect. The slightest pressure will be felt and obeyed by some, while others need the strongest possible use of the leg to galvanise them into activity!

The Weight of the Body

The weight of the body will not be much used as an aid by the beginner. Suffice to say here that it will help the horse if the rider keeps her body in balance; and that, should she wish to turn to either side, she can indicate this to her horse by inclining her body in the direction in which she wishes to turn, his natural reaction to the displacement of the weight he is carrying being to turn in the direction of that displacement.

The Hands

The hands take part in our conversation with our horse by acting through the reins and the bit on his mouth. (It is not proposed in this book to go into the subject of bits and bitting; but it is helpful if the reader knows the broad principles of the subject.)

For all ordinary work the reins should be held in both hands.

When riding in a bridle with one rein only, the rein may be held between the third and fourth finger or round the outside of the little finger, and brought across the palm of the hand and out and forward again over the top of the first finger. With a bridle with two reins the lower rein may be brought round the outside of the little finger, across the palm of the hand, and out over the top of the first finger; while the top reins may be held between the second and third finger and also brought out over the top of the first finger.

With the reins held thus the rider will find that, by turning her wrist so that her little finger draws nearer to her body, she can tighten the lower rein while loosening the upper rein; but, as the latter has the milder action of the two on the horse's mouth, for all ordinary purposes she should try to use the upper rein in preference to the lower.

If the rider holds the reins in place with the fingers rather than with the thumb she will find that it increases the flexibility of her wrists, as the tightening of the thumb seems to have a stiffening effect on the wrist.

If the reins are all taken into one hand the rider must be particularly careful to adjust them so that the reins on one side are neither longer nor shorter than those on the other, and so that she has a level feel on her horse's mouth. A simple method of ensuring this if, for example, all the reins are being taken into the left hand, is to slip the right reins through the fingers so that they are a little longer than the left, at the same time placing them over the first finger of the left hand and down the palm, so that the left hand grasps them at exactly the same spot at which they were held by the right hand. The rider will then find that her reins are of equal length, but that, by turning her wrist, she can instantly bring more or less bearing on either side of her horse's mouth.

There are many good ways of holding the reins, of which the three methods given here are only examples. As long as the rider can use all four reins singly or in their various combinations to their best advantage the way in which she holds them matters little.

Broadly speaking, there are two methods of guiding a horse with the reins.

The first is by "feeling" the rein on the side towards which we want to turn, bending our horse's head in that direction.

The second is by using the opposite rein – the right rein for instance, to go to the left, and *vice versa* – and pressing it against, or drawing it across, our horse's neck towards whichever side we want to turn. When we do this the trained horse will move away from the pressure of the rein on his neck and turn in the required direction.

When we are riding quietly along, "at ease", we can do so with a long rein, guiding our horse merely by the touch of the rein on his neck, or by using our weight as a tight-rope walker uses his balancing pole. But when we are riding "at attention" our hands should be in touch with our horse's mouth, maintaining the lightest and smoothest feeling consistent with control, and giving their instructions as gently as possible. This touch between horse and rider has, for want of a better word, been called "contact". But contact is not a good term, for to many people it seems to imply a constant dead pressure, and nothing is more tiring to a horse or more ruinous to his training than a dead pressure on his mouth. But with a loose connection between wire and terminal, sparks fly between the two. It is, not a perpetually tight rein, nor actual pressure, but a sympathetic understanding and preparedness; and when trouble is in the offing, reins short enough for control to be applied without any suddenness or jerk. Occasionally, of course, it may be found necessary to use the hands quite strongly to enforce obedience, and when this is so we need not hesitate to be firm; control is of primary importance, gentleness of secondary; nevertheless, the two should be combined whenever possible.

It should always be realised that a horse in a state of collection, a term which we will explain later, is so to speak "teed-up", and it must inevitably be fatiguing to him if kept up indefinitely. It is essential, therefore, to his temper and training, no less than to his muscles, that he be given ample periods of relief. Let him walk with a long, loose rein whenever circumstances permit, and when standing still, let him lower his head and be free to stretch his neck, and rest all those muscles which will work for us all the more readily if they are fresh. It is a fact, too, that for anatomical reasons, a horse cannot walk fast with long, easy strides unless he is allowed to extend his neck, which in turn allows him to extend his shoulders. Experience shows that beginners have a tendency to hold on to their horse's head much too tightly at this pace, and they should, therefore, be careful to ride with sufficient length of rein.

Lightness, then, should be our aim, and we should feel our horse's mouth through the reins almost as a pianist feels the piano. For those lovely, light, rippling passages only the fingers work in all their wonderful flexibility; for stronger music perhaps the wrists come into play, and for the great, powerful chords even the forearm is called upon to work. On your light, resilient horse with his mouth of silk, what need to use more than the fingers?

To stop many horses no more than a "fixing" of the fingers is necessary, but for others there must be an increased tension on the reins. On a horse that is setting his jaw and pulling hard, the rider will find that if she pulls first one rein and then the other, bringing the pressure of the bit from side to side of the horse's mouth (the same sort of idea as when drawing her towel backwards and forwards across her back to dry it) it will have far more effect in making him relax his muscles than a dead pull, however strong. To make it effective she must not loosen one rein when she is pulling the other, but pull one against the other. She should never use this action, however, unless it is necessary. Many people, having discovered how effective it is, will often use it when a smooth feel or a little sympathetic, intermittent vibration of the fingers would have attained the desired result. When used unnecessarily it tends to irritate the horse and spoil his mouth. When a horse walks, trots or canters he moves his head and neck slightly from side to side in rhythm with his body movement.

"Keep the hands still." Yes! but still in relation to the horse's mouth, not in relation to our own body. If, at the trot, the shoulders and elbows are kept stiff, the hands will probably be perfectly still in relation to our own body, but far from still in relation to the horse's mouth. As the body rises and falls the reins will loosen and tighten and rub up and down on his neck, and the bit will move continuously and unsympathetically in his mouth. This will not worry the strong-mouthed horse, but will cause discomfort to one whose mouth is very light. Let the joints of our arms and hands have natural play, and see, as an exercise, how still we can keep the reins on our horse's neck and the bit in his mouth.

At the canter the beginner finds it even harder to keep her hands quiet than she does at the trot. As the horse's forehand is raised the distance between his mouth and her hand is decreased, and as it goes down, his nose goes out and the full length of rein is required. It will therefore be realised that if the shoulder and the elbow joints are kept stiff, the reins will be tightening and loosening at every stride, an irritating and uncomfortable performance for the horse. It can be avoided by allowing the joints of the fingers, wrists, elbows, and shoulders to have free play. This may, perhaps, better be expressed by asking the beginner to imagine that her hands are attached to her coat buttons by a very weak piece of elastic, and that she allows the horse and the elastic to move them, so that the downward movement of the horse's head stretches the elastic, and the elastic brings the hands back again as the horse's head comes up. It is a continuous and smooth movement, the elastic taking over control of the hands at the very moment the horse's mouth no longer requires them to yield, and the feel on the mouth being as light as the elastic is weak.

Now let the beginner substitute the muscles of the fingers, wrists, arms, and shoulders for the elastic, and remember that these muscles, like the elastic, should yield and allow the hands to be drawn forward by the movement of the horse's head; and then, without a break in the movement, draw them back again as the horse's head starts to rise. Thus a perfectly smooth and very light feel can be maintained on the horse's mouth; but mind that it *is* light; better no feeling at all than one that is heavy.

How true is the old saying that there are three types of

"hands", bad hands, no hands, and good hands; "hands" being used to describe that subtle management of the reins that is so hard to define.

The woman with no "hands" can ride a certain number of horses most successfully. Her security of seat allows her to leave her horse's head entirely alone, and this she does, never interfering with him, but, at the same time, never being of much help to him and being unable to exert that control which is needed to ride a difficult horse.

But the woman with good "hands" not only has that security of seat, but possesses also the knowledge and sensitiveness which allow her to use the aids with tact and strength, and to ride the most awkward horses.

"Hands" or the possibility of develping them are entirely lacking in some people, but in most people they are there to a larger or smaller degree to be cultivated by practice, study, and imagination.

Beginners, till they have developed a good seat and gained a thorough knowledge of the aids, would be wise not to use their hands for more than the simplest indications. It would be like trying to run before being able to walk. The use of the hands is much too subtle a thing to attempt too soon. Seat comes first; then the ability to keep a smooth, light feel on the horse's mouth at all paces and not until these have been acquired should an "active" use of the hands be attempted. Many a horse has been temporarily spoilt by the constant nagging of a rider who has learned a little but not enough.

The Voice

In controlling certain horses the voice is of assistance. Talking quietly to them often has a soothing effect, while a low scolding voice (never shouting) will sometimes turn obstinacy into acquiescence. A horse may also be taught to obey words of command.

Artificial Aids

The whip, the spur, martingales, etc., are generally classified as "artificial aids".

In the side-saddle the whip, applied with a smooth pressure or gentle taps on the horse's off-side, can be used as a substitute for the rider's leg on that side of her horse; but it is only in the more complicated movements that it need thus be used.

The whip can also be used as a punishment; but as more horses are marred than made by its wrong use we should do well, throughout our whole careers as horsewomen, to think twice before resorting to it. A whole chapter could be written on its use and abuse; even the way to carry it and its "picking up" so that it is held in such a way as to be an efficient instrument, require thought and instruction; while every horse and every circumstance need different treatment. A beginner will never do harm by leaving it unused during differences of opinion with her horse, whereas by its use at the wrong moment or in the wrong way, she may set up mental resistances which may take months to overcome.

The spur is a reserve force which the rider has at her disposal if the horse does not answer to the pressure of the leg. It should not be fitted with rowels, and should only be worn by those who have enough knowledge to use it with justice, and enough control over their leg to be sure that they never use it unintentionally.

Part Four
Schooling

CHAPTER V

Turns at the Halt and in Movement. Lateral Movements

Turning our horse in the direction in which we wish to go or the making of small changes of position when standing still may seem to be simple matters, but in reality they contain many points of importance that require consideration.

A horse may turn in one of three ways: he may pivot about his forehand, about his centre, or about his haunches. That is to say, he may use his forelegs as a pivot and swing his quarters round his legs till he faces in the required direction, in which case he is said to have turned on the forehand; or he may turn his forehand towards a new direction and swing his quarters round to correspond, when he will have turned on his centre; or he may use his hindlegs as the pivot and swing his forehand round in the direction in which he is to turn, this being called a turn on the haunches or Pirouette. In doing this he pivots about the inner hindleg. For a turn to the right the rider must guide her horse with the right rein supported by the left, but this left rein should be used with care, for if it is applied too strongly it will nullify the effect of the direct rein, an error almost invariably committed by beginners. At the same time enough rein should be applied to keep up impulsion, check any backward movement and prevent the horse's quarters swinging out to the left. When making this movement the rider will find that her horse has a strong tendency to move his haunches, for turning on them correctly is not an easy movement to carry out, and it is only after some training that he will turn readily in this manner. When turning the forehand round to the left the rider may find that she has to use the pressure of her whip on the off-side, for the indirect rein of opposition behind the withers may be insufficient to prevent her horse's quarters swinging out in that direction.

The turn on the forehand is one extreme and the turn on the haunches is the other. Between them lie all the gradations of the turn on the centre, ranging from a turn about a point just behind the forehand to one about a point just in front of the haunches. When in movement, for most practical purposes turns are done on the centre, but the sharper the turn and the greater the spin the more will the rider feel that she needs to get her horse's hocks under him and place his weight more on the haunches than on the forehand. It is an unpleasant sensation, and unsafe, to feel the horse's quarters flying out, almost as though they would swing him off his forelegs or make him cross them or slip up. To turn comfortably therefore, and I make so bold as to say correctly, at any but a slow pace, the rider must have her horse balanced and collected; and to prevent that alarming swing out of the quarters, she must use the same aids as she would for the pivot on the haunches at the halt. To do this, as forward movement is being maintained, she will obtain a wide balanced turn on the centre.

As soon as she has mastered the turn on the haunches at the halt, the would-be learner may turn her attention to lateral movements, which is a term used to describe all movements of a horse to the side, or to the side and forward, with his forelegs and hindlegs making parallel tracks. Although in practice lateral movements will generally be used only for small adjustments of position such as moving nearer to a gate or closing up to or passing away from another person, in the show ring today every hack is expected to be able to execute them correctly. The two most commonly used lateral movements are the half passage and the full passage, the former when we wish to move to one side and forward, and the latter when we wish to move directly to one side. There are others, but it will suffice if I give certain general principles and describe in detail the two mentioned.

In the right half pass the horse moves forward and to the right, his forelegs and hindlegs making parallel tracks and his path making an angle of 45 degrees with the original direction. His body should be inclined to the right only just enough to allow his near-fore and near-hind to cross in front of his off-fore and off-hind, respectively, and he should be bent from the poll very slightly in the direction in which he is moving.

In the full passage to the right the horse moves to the right, but not forward, or shall we say not perceptibly forward – *i.e.*, in a path at right angles to his original direction – again with his body inclined very slightly to the right.

In the left half passage and full passage to the left the movements are, of course, similar, but in the reverse direction and with the horse's off-fore and off-hind crossing in front of his near-fore and near-hind.

In all lateral movements the forehand should incline to a greater or lesser degree in the direction of the movement, or, in other words, should precede the quarters and the legs should cross in front of and not behind their fellows. Also the horse's head should be bent from the poll very slightly in the direction in which he is moving.

These conditions ensure that there is sufficient impulsion and that the rider has her horse in control "between her leg and hand". If there is insufficient impulsion the horse will be behind the bit, and, supposing he is passaging to the right, he may swing his quarters out to the right, crossing his legs one behind the other and in a sense his quarters will be preceding his forehand. Another advantage of having the head correctly bent is that it ensures that the horse can look where he is going.

To perform a lateral movement to the right the rider should "lead" her horse's forehand with the right rein, supported by the left rein. She should use her leg to keep up the impulsion and to make her horse pass his quarters away to the right. Here again it is very important that she should not use the supporting rein so strongly that the effect of the right rein is nullified and her horse's head is bent to the left, putting him in a faulty position and dissipating the impulsion.

To carry out a correct lateral movement to the left the rider may have to employ her whip on the off-side; but, with a highly trained horse it is possible so to balance the use of the left rein with that of the right indirect rein of opposition behind the withers, that the former will lead the horse to the left and bend him in that direction, while the latter will move his quarters to the left in such a way that the bend of his head to the left from the poll is preserved, and the horse executes the movement correctly in every detail.

When the beginner has become proficient in the execution of lateral movements I think she will appreciate more deeply than before how valuable to her is the use of the right rein applied to oppose the forehand to the quarters. In this way she can definitely produce or limit certain movements of the horse's hindquarters, and thus, on many occasions, make use of her reins to take the place of the leg which she would have on the off-side of her horse were she riding astride.

CHAPTER VI

The Reins. Their names and their effects

It is an important part of the training of a side-saddle horse that he should be taught the language of the rein aids. As has been discussed at some length, the side-saddle rider may use many of the same aids as an astride rider, but of course the weight distribution is different, and has to be counteracted into balance, by careful adjustment of the way in which a rider sits on her saddle; then there is the absence of the rider's leg on the "off" side. Thus the more important role of the rein aids becomes apparent.

I propose to name the rein aids and their effects as taught by the French masters of equitation, because I believe these to be most relevant to the application of side-saddle riding. However, in this day and age there are many good trainers who use methods from Germany, Scandinavia, Vienna, to say nothing of Spain and Portugal. So, suffice to say a horse *can* be trained through many methods – the important thing is that he answers the aids he has been taught.

So, to the rein aids, French style:

1. The Direct Rein.
2. The Opening Rein.
3. The In-direct Rein in front of the withers.
4. The In-direct Rein behind the withers.
5. The Neck Rein.

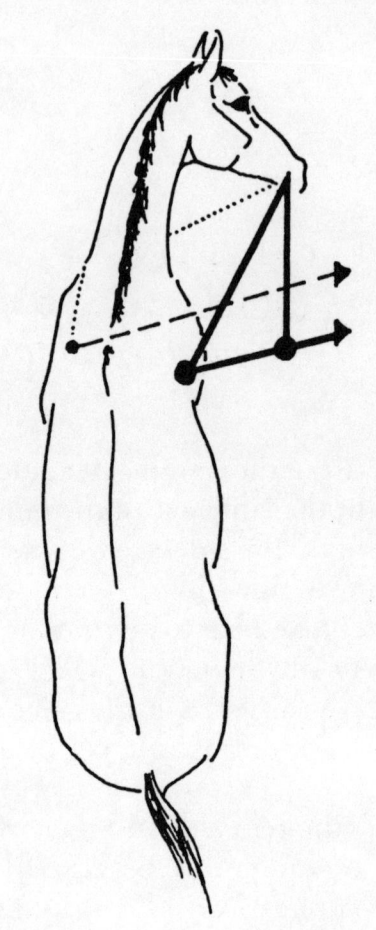

THE OPENING REIN
To show position, action and effect of this rein aid in side-saddle

1. The continuous line from the horse's mouth to the large dot shows the position of the opening rein to the hand. There are two right hand positions shown, the one nearest the horse's neck is the one of lesser degree of effect (for a fully schooled horse); the one furthest from the horse's neck is for a less well schooled horse

2. The smaller dots indicate the supporting hand

3. The arrow pointing to the right on the continuous line shows the continued effect of the opening rein

4. The broken line from the small dot shows the direction in which the horse's weight is displaced thus, with no leg aids, causing the horse to turn his shoulders to the right

THE REINS

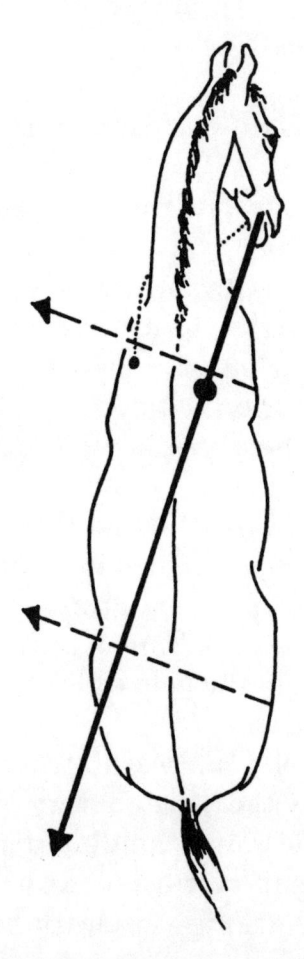

THE INDIRECT REIN (used behind the withers)
To show position, action and effect of this rein aid in side-saddle

1. The continuous line shows the position of the rein, and the large dot the position of the acting hand

2. The smaller dots indicate the supporting hand

3. The broken line from the right shoulder and right hip of the horse shows the effect the rein has, and the direction the horse will move in, i.e. as this (right) rein is used it will cause a displacement of the horse's body weight to the left, which without the right leg aid, will make the horse's quarters move around his shoulders – thus turning on the forehand

The effects of the reins:

1. *The Direct Rein.* Used to steady, or stop a horse, also helps in direct flexion. Close fingers on both reins fairly tightly, but do not pull backwards unless absolutely necessary.
2. *The Opening Rein.* Used to turn a horse (including Pirouette at walk and Half-Pass). If turning right, carry both hands to the right, the left one stays near the left side of the horse's neck, whilst the right hand and forearm move out towards a position where in astride riding the rider's right knee would be. If the horse is not very well schooled then the hand may have to come out four or five inches (10 to 12 cm), if he is well schooled then an inch (2·5 cm) will suffice. The rider must remember not to lean or tip over, only to move the hands and arms.
3. *The Indirect Rein used in front of the withers.* Used to turn a horse round without the help of leg aids. As is the one used behind the withers.

    There is however a subtle difference in that the one used in front of the withers has a very strong effect on the displacement of the horse's hindquarters to the side. Making the horse, in effect, perform a turn on the centre. Front feet and hindfeet each making a circle (or half circle) around the horse's centre axis.

    The rider in using the right rein in front of the withers keeps her left hand softly against the horse's neck whilst the right hand brings the right rein across the horse's neck, and at the same time slightly back towards the left pommel.
4. *The indirect rein used behind the withers.* This rein causes displacement of the horse's quarters, but allows the forehand to stay put, thus causing a turn on the forehand.

    The rider uses the reins in the same way as for the No. 3, but brings the hand back towards the centre button of her riding coat.

    In my opinion this is a most important rein to use and to

understand. It is not difficult to use – most horses will respond to it straightaway.

5. *The Neck rein.* Used to turn a horse when holding the reins in only one hand. If, for instance, one wishes to turn a horse to the right, and is holding both reins in the left hand – which being the "bridle" hand is often the case – one should have an even rein contact with the horse's mouth, and at the same time carry the left hand until it and the left rein are touching the left side of the horse's neck. This puts more weight onto the horse's right shoulder and he will, himself, follow this weight displacement

I will not go into greater detail – if the rider wishes to consult one of the many excellent publications on equitation a much deeper study may be made. Suffice to say that in the application of all aids, kindness and clarity are paramount and the "acting" rein is the one which does the work, whilst the "supporting" rein does just that – supports its neighbour.

All reins can be supported also to a degree by the rider's left leg and by the subtle application of a long whip on the right side or "off" side, just to keep the horse's attention, sometimes described as keeping him "up to the bit".

CHAPTER VII

Cantering with a named leg and Flying change of leg

Owing to the complexity and often controversy over the correct aids for cantering a horse on a particular lead, it is important to discuss these aids only in the context of side-saddle riding. Even though I also advise side-saddle riders to read one of the many excellent books now available on equitation so as to study the canter as a whole. In a previous chapter a rider has been told how to sit in a side-saddle at canter, but not actually how to ask the horse to break into canter. (See Chapter III.)

When describing in detail the aids to make a horse strike-off as desired, we cannot be dogmatic. The point is to put him into the easiest and most correct position for him to lead with the required leg; to hold him in that position; and then to ask him to strike off at the *right moment*. Any aids which will attain this object may be said to be correct.

To reiterate: the essentials for making a horse strike off on a named leg are:

1. To place him in a position from which it is easy for him to lead as desired (corner of a riding school, for instance).
2. To hold him together (*i.e.*, in both balance and pace) until he has broken into a canter.
3. To ask him to strike off at the psychological moment. (This

is very important indeed, especially when bearing in mind that a horse strikes off in a slightly different way and time, out of trot than out of walk.)

I should like to consider the above points a little more. When talking of positioning a horse, there is his bodily position and the use of a place such as the corner of a riding arena in which to use the bodily position. In canter the horse's shoulder on the "leading" side must be freed of some weight, *i.e.*, when travelling to the right the rider displaces some more weight to the left, turns (very slightly) the horse's neck to the left – not necessarily his whole head and neck, thus creating a "wrong bend", but just enough to ease the horse's position. The horse must then be held together, *i.e.*, balanced, and if travelling to the right the usual diagonal canter aid may be applied with the left leg and right (acting) rein. However, when cantering left this is not so easy because of the lack of a right leg. So the horse must be kept well-balanced and going forward from the leg, and if necessary on a young or un-schooled horse the whip may be used as a substitute leg, and the aid is thus much the same as normal (*i.e.*, diagonal). However, on a well schooled horse the rein aids come into play and one should be able to teach the horse to obey a feel on the left rein for canter left and vice versa. *This is where timing, patience and skill all play a part.*

To change the canter lead via the "flying" change the timing of the aids is of vital importance. Let us take as an example the case of a horse leading with the near fore and we wish then to change onto the off-fore. This can for simplicity's sake be divided into three periods, the sequence of the stride before the "change" is: off-hind (first period), near hind and off-fore (second period), near fore (third period). The horse now changes behind, and the next leg to come to the ground is the near hind, followed by the off-hind; then, having changed in front (the changing behind and in front being nearly simultaneous), the near fore; and finally the new leading leg (the off-fore). All this should happen in one smooth continuous movement.

In applying the aid at the correct moment we can assume that a correct change begins during the third period, this means that with the average horse he should receive the aid before the third period commences, which, borne out by close observation, means that the rider should apply the aid during the second period, when the near-hind and off-fore (the diagonal) is on the ground; and if the change is to be made from off-fore to near-fore *vice versa*. (This right to left change is more difficult in the side-saddle because of the weight variation and distribution, but can be quite easily perfected with practise.)

There are a number of faults such as changing in front only – or behind only (less frequent) – which may be attributed to either the horse not being ready in his schooling to perform the movement or by a rider mis-timing her aids and sometimes a combination of both.

In Victorian days and even later, a lady's horse to be perfect had always to canter with the off-fore leading. Possibly this was due to the cramped position often adopted in those days. However, it is true that when a horse is cantering, his body is not following an entirely straight line, the hind feet do not always follow exactly the track of the front feet, and can on a long or rough striding horse lead to a rather rolling gait which is uncomfortable especially in a side-saddle. If the horse is leading on the near-fore he canters into his rider's legs, so to speak, and away from them when on the off-fore. In a well-schooled horse this tendency to lean or roll can be counteracted by a good free going and at the same time well-balanced canter.

Part Five
Jumping

CHAPTER VIII

Jumping. Movements of the Horse when Jumping. Effect on Rider's Seat. Swing. The Leaping Head on the Saddle. Hands when Jumping. Being "Left"

I think it is fair to say that a "balanced" or "forward" seat is now accepted world-wide. The priority in jumping a fence whilst riding side-saddle is to be "balanced". Which point Mrs Archer Houblon has concluded from our analysis.

First, let us try and analyse the movements of a horse over a fence. It is interesting at the beginning to note how, at the last stride before jumping, a horse lowers his head apparently to look more carefully at the fence, but in reality, I suspect to allow greater play to all his jumping muscles, the full use of which is partly regulated by the muscles of his neck.

We see that the initial spring, or, shall we say, the initial movement, of the take-off, comes from the forelegs, the leading leg in canter (in this case the near fore) starting to raise the forehand almost before the hindlegs have come to the ground, and in the next instant, however, the horse's hindlegs take the weight, and, helped by an extension of the head and neck, the muscles of his loins, hindquarters, and hocks take him, as would a spring, further up and over the fence. So, the term "take-off" really covers the whole period between horse's forelegs giving the first upward impulse to the forehand and the moment when, with hindlegs extended, his hind toes leave the ground. Having taken off, he describes a curve through the air and lands first on one foreleg and then on the other, and glides into the next stride so smoothly and lightly that it almost seems as if the forelegs leave the ground again before the hindlegs land.

How would these movements of the horse affect an inanimate object placed upon the saddle? The effect would be that the "punch" with which he launches his own weight over the fence would shoot that object far and fast into the air! How well do those who, in their youth, tried to jump astride without being taught to get forward remember how helpless they felt to cope with that dreaded hoist!

Now take the case of some hapless beginner put up in a side-saddle and asked to jump a large fence before she has practised over small ones. As she approaches the obstacle her body is stiff and leaning slightly back as though anticipating some horrid shock (as indeed she is!); when the horse raises his forehead to jump she is tilted still further back; and then, when he leaves the ground, the whole weight of her rigid body being planted well on the seat of the saddle, she receives through her seat the full force of his spring. She is only saved from being shot clean into the air by her pommels and by the reins to which she clings in desperation. It is an unpleasant performance for her, and even worse for her horse, whose every movement is impeded by the bouncing of her weight on his back and by the pull on his mouth, which wrenches his head into the air just when he most needs full freedom from restraint. How therefore can we prevent this?

Let us examine carefully the first part of a jump. We should approach the fence sitting in our normal position, balanced and moving in rhythm with our horse; as his forelegs leave the ground we should swing our body forward – so far forward that we keep in touch and balance not only with the rising of his foreleg, but also with the increased velocity due to his spring; and then if we have made our swing with sufficient generosity we will find that our centre of gravity is moved right forward up to the front of our saddle, and our seat is, so to speak, "rolled up" and forward until it is no longer in direct contact with the seat of the saddle, *i.e.*, the forward or balanced position. Thus when the force of the horse's spring is developed through hocks, quarters, and loins, we will find that we are not "sitting on the punch", but are securely poised on the forepart of the saddle, as impervious to shock as is a really well-sprung car to the ordinary incidents of the roadway.

The key, then, to the balanced jump at which we are aiming – the jump in which we get no shock or jerk and do not interfere with our horse – lies in our weight, during our horse's upward movement, being poised through our right thigh on the forepart of the saddle. The effect of this is twofold. It allows us to be really "with" our horse during the jump, and it brings our seat clear of the saddle so that we avoid the shock of his spring. There is no need, however, to think of these two effects separately, for both are obtained by swinging the body forward. In fact, we cannot obtain the one without the other. If, while the horse is tilted upwards in the first stage of his jump, we are leaning forward so that the whole weight is poised over our horse's centre of gravity, then our seat cannot be in the saddle. It is anatomically impossible. It follows, therefore, that we need only concentrate on our forward swing, and, if this is in perfect timing *and sufficiently generous to carry our weight to the right place*, it will also take our seat out of the saddle. And so we may say that in the forward swing, carried out so as to obtain these two effects, lies the secret of a really pleasant jump in a side-saddle.

It is not easy, of course, for the beginner to time the horse's take-off correctly, or to swing forward vigorously enough to be really "with" him over the fence. I strongly advocate practising this "swinging" movement by horse and rider walking over a pole on the ground before graduating to a low, single jump and before even attempting a longer fence. As he approaches it, therefore, she must keep in close touch and rhythm, and, with her eyes on the fence ahead, concentrate on his movements, the more accurately to judge the instant at which he will begin to take off. At that instant, neither a moment before nor after, she must, until practise has taught her to do so without thought, make a conscious effort to swing forward, and so to ensure that she is going with her horse throughout the jump.

It is important that she should swing from the very seat, the bend coming from below and not above the hipbone, from where the leg joins the body. If it merely comes from the waist it only affects the upper part of the body and does not bring the whole of her weight forward, so that she is left "behind" her horse and to the mercy of his "punch".

While the horse is landing the rider's body automatically reverts to its normal position for forward movement – that is to say, just in front of the perpendicular. For the normal jump the beginner should not think about swinging her body back as she lands. Such thought generally detracts from the vigour of the forward swing, brings the body back too soon and too much, and results in an unbalanced jump. If her body is in the right place for the first half of the jump, it will, of itself, in all ordinary circumstances, remain in balance for the rest; while, if the horse leaves his hindlegs in a ditch, or if for any other reason the rider wishes to alter her balance, she will find that she has her body in such control that she can do so without difficulty.

It is very easy to get into the habit of swinging the body out to the left as well as forward, and this is a fault against which we must be on our guard. We should go forward perfectly straight.

Some people, after swinging their body forward correctly, will let it describe a sort of circular movement to the left as it swings back. This fault also is, of course, to be avoided.

Many beginners are puzzled because they land with a bump and with their bodies crouching over their horse's withers. They think it is because they have swung too far forward on taking off, whereas, in reality, it is either because they have been the fraction of a second late and too stiff, or have not swung forward far enough, with the result that they have failed to avoid the force of the horse's spring and have been shot forward involuntarily.

Throughout the jump the left knee should keep supple and in its place on the saddle. The lower part of the leg should not be allowed to move appreciably forwards or backwards, but it will, owing to the suppleness of the knee, sometimes be found to swing outwards and upwards away from the horse's side as he is landing, just as our handkerchief floats out if we hold it by the corner and rapidly lower our hand.

The suppleness of the knee is also very important in that it must allow the thigh to pivot forward, so that the rider's seat can come right off the saddle and her weight move to its right place while the horse is rising. But here we are confronted with a difficulty. It will be noticed that when the thigh pivots forward in this way above the knee, the distance it moves is much greater near the hip than near the knee, so that, *assuming that the leaping head is placed at a distance of a thickness of a hand from the thigh*, the higher up it is placed the more is the forward movement restricted, and the lower down it is placed, the greater is the range of movement allowed to the upper part of the thigh. Now, the prevailing leaping head of today comes halfway up the thigh, so that forward movement beyond a certain point is arrested, and it is impossible for the rider to keep her knee in its place on the saddle and yet to get her weight really far enough forward when jumping anything but a small fence. A rider can make every endeavour to get forward, even going to the length of letting her knee move right back on the saddle so as to allow her thigh to rotate round the leaping head. Yet, though she has succeeded in getting her seat out of the saddle during the first stage of the jump, her whole weight is still "behind" her horse, and in another instance she seems almost to have slipped over the back of her saddle. In yet another case she loses her stirrup. That in itself is of little consequence, but in this particular case it is an indication that something is wrong with her seat over the fence.

As a matter of fact, all these problems are caused by the rider trying her utmost to get as far forward as she would were she riding astride; but each time she was impeded by the broad pommel placed on the saddle in such a way as to make it impossible to attain a correct position or balance.

This common position of the leaping head, it is true, gives the rider firmness of seat when she is "left behind" her horse over a fence, or when he is "playing up". She can grip up under it, and, though it may necessitate her remaining "behind" her horse while so doing, it does help her to avoid being shot up from the saddle.

Can this disadvantage of the usual leaping head be overcome? Can we have one that will fulfil a dual rôle, a pommel that, without preventing us from getting our weight right forward in the saddle over a large fence, will give us support when in that position, and also be so shaped and placed that we can grip up against it if we find ourselves in difficulties and "behind our horse"? We can. It is a leaping head made by Messrs. Mayhew, which I feel I must mention as it is the only solution to the problem that I know. When buying a side-saddle it is important to ask the make. Mayhew saddles are available second-hand still and ask if the saddle you are looking at has a "Mayhew" type leaping head pommel. It is different from the usual leaping head, both in its placing on the saddle and shape. Firstly, it is placed further forward and lower down, still with only the thickness of the hand between it and the thigh, but not so low that we feel insecure or in danger of our knee being drawn above it. Placing it thus brings it nearer to the knee, so that this clearance of the thickness of the hand is sufficient to allow ample range of movement to the thigh and enables us to swing our weight right forward over a fence without any displacement of the knee. Secondly, so that the thigh shall have support when in the extreme forward position as well as when gripping up, it is made with the usual wide undersurface bent so as to present half its width to be engaged by an upward grip of the thigh when we find ourselves "behind our horse" and in difficulties, and the rear half so that it faces towards and gives support to the thigh when the body is in the extreme forward position. This bending upwards of the undersurface of the pommel appreciably narrows the width that engages the thigh at any one time, and so gives still further freedom of movement to our forward swing. The exact position in which it is fixed on the saddle depends, of course, largely on the build of the rider. This leaping head allows us to assume a better position over a fence.

Now let us consider the hands. In all ordinary circumstances the rider should aim at keeping a light and perfectly smooth feel on her horse's mouth throughout the jump. This is dictated, not by any need of the horse for "support" or otherwise during his jump, but by the difficulty of regaining touch once it has been lost without giving him some degree of jerk on the mouth. Clearly the maintenance of touch will necessitate some adjustment of the position of the hands in relation to the body as the rider swings forward. If her arms remain rigid the distance between her hands and the horse's mouth will decrease, the reins will sag, and touch will be lost. She must, therefore, bend her arms as her body goes forward so that the reins are kept taut and a light feel is maintained. As her body swings back in the course of the jump she should allow her hands to be drawn forward and down, perhaps to their full extent; in fact, she may even have to extend her fingers to give the necessary freedom to her horse's head.

She must be careful not to snatch her hands back as her body goes forward, or to push them out independently as the horse is landing; she should allow them to respond as lightly as possible to every movement of her horse's head and neck from take-off to landing.

If she finds that her hands tend to jerk up as she is landing it is a sure sign that she has been stiff and was "left" as her horse took off. Remove the cause by improving the swing, the tendency will disappear, and the rider will find that she can with ease let her hands go forward and down as she lands, thus giving her horse all the freedom he requires.

Hitherto we have only been considering the jump when everything goes well, but what of the many times when we are "left"? It may be that our horse takes off a whole stride too soon. Small wonder that we are caught unawares! Or perhaps he is coming wrong into his fence and we are uncertain whether he will stand back, will put in a short stride, or will get too close under it. Often this uncertainty causes us to lose our rhythm and our horse jumps away from us. An error on our part, no doubt, but after all we are only human beings! Or, again, we may be on a "sticky" horse, or even telling the owner of a keen little head and a pair of pricked ears that beyond the fence ahead lies a great big ditch. In the last two cases we are sitting down and riding till our horse takes off, and in so doing we put our weight a little behind the normal as explained earlier. These are circumstances in which I think we can scarcely avoid being "left". I have yet to discover the woman who is quick enough to get really with her horse over a fence, having been behind him when he took off. Let us, therefore, examine how best to overcome the difficulties of such a situation. If we are "left" only because we are sitting down and "driving" our horse, we are in such close touch with him that it is possible we may not be caught unawares by his spring. In this case we may be "left" so slightly that there will be no hesitation in the movement of our body as he takes off; our forward swing, though "behind" him, will yet be supple, and we will remain comfortably seated in the saddle, though with that unsatisfactory feeling of jumping the fence "behind" and not "with" our horse. The effect of being thoroughly well "left" is more difficult to deal with, but still it can to some extent be overcome. Here we have to employ every means in our power to keep our seat. We should bring our reserve grip into action, and at the same time we should relax the muscles and joints of the upper part of our body, so that it "collapses", so to speak, and presents the minimum amount of resistance to the upward

Plate 24 CAVALLETTI AT TROT
Showing the forward bend of the rider's body.

Plate 25 A SMALL FENCE
Also showing the rider in forward position and in balance with the horse's movement.

Plate 26 TAKING OFF (off-side)
Rider's body swinging well forward so that her weight is over the point of balance.

Plate 31 LANDING (near-side)
Rider adjusting to horse landing well out from the fence. Lower left leg slightly forward and body upright, hands keeping an even contact with horse's mouth via the reins (no backward tension).

Plate 30 IN THE AIR (near-side)
Rider's body well "folded" over right thigh, weight in left stirrup iron.

Plate 27 IN THE AIR (off-side)
Rider's body right forward and really going with the horse, note the arm and hand allowing horse to stretch his head and neck to the full.

Plate 28 LANDING (off-side)
Rider's body returning to normal position.

Plate 29 TAKE-OFF (near-side)
Rider's weight well forward and seat off the side. The Rider's left thigh is up against the leaping head whilst the right lower leg and heel are close to the left shin bone.

Plate 32 OVER THE JUMP (near-side)
A horse travelling at speed and jumping a hedge, showing the horse using himself to the maximum, with the rider poised over the point of balance.

Plate 33 OVER THE JUMP (off-side)
Again a horse galloping on and jumping a ditch and hedge, horse and rider in harmony. Note the similarity of the rider's position to that of No. 23.

MOVEMENTS OF THE HORSE WHEN JUMPING

thrust of the horse's spring. Our natural tendency is to stiffen, in which case our body will neither swing forwards nor backwards, and we will be shot upwards, leaving only two alternatives, that of falling off or keeping our seat at the expense of the horse's mouth. This collapsing of our body, therefore, is most important.

And what of our hands? As our horse is jumping "away" from us our initial length of rein will become insufficient as he extends his neck, and at all costs we must avoid hitting him in the mouth or preventing the free movement of his head. So we should relax our fingers, and let the reins slip through them, if necessary to the buckle. Then, as he lands, we should draw the reins back towards our body with one hand, take them in the other hand further forwards, and then adjust them in both hands at the necessary length for control. Thus, if we can but relax instead of stiffening, and instead of holding them tight, slip our reins, and that not so grudgingly that our horse has to drag them from our hands, we will get a jump which is passably smooth and comfortable both for us and for our horse. It must, however, be understood that it falls short of the ideal in that it can never give us that feeling of exhilaration and oneness with our horse that is so thrilling in a perfectly balanced jump; further, our weight, being behind the horse's centre of gravity, will not be ideally placed for him to carry it over the fence; and, having had to slip our reins, we will not be in the best position to control him the instant he lands.

Fear of hurting our horse's mouth over a fence may sometimes tempt us to do what might also be described as throwing the reins over in front of him; and, on a horse that has lost confidence through rough handling of the reins, this is no bad practice till his fears have been banished. But it must not be done until he has actually taken off, and it must be done sufficiently generously to ensure him complete freedom of head from take-off to landing. In the first place, if we suddenly loosen the reins before he has started to jump, especially on a horse that likes to be held in balance when coming into a fence, it may disconcert him and make him jump badly or refuse. In the second, if the reins are lengthened insufficiently and we are not prepared to slip them further the instant more rein is demanded, we will almost certainly hit our horse in the mouth when he extends his neck.

If a horse pecks on landing the rider should endeavour to sit as quietly as a mouse, just trying to keep in balance, and allowing the reins to slip through her fingers so that he may have complete freedom of head to balance and recover. She cannot help him by "picking him up" with her reins. How can you possibly "pick up", or lift, anything on top of which you are sitting? If attempted it will only impede the horse's efforts not to fall.

Appendices

APPENDIX I

Mounting and Dismounting

There are several good ways of mounting when riding side-saddle, but the one which will, I think, be found most generally useful is to mount as though astride and then to bring the right leg across into position. This makes the rider as little dependent on help from another person as it is possible to be, and, therefore, is workmanlike, though perhaps not so graceful as other methods.

If the horse is so tall that it is difficult for the rider to get her foot up into the stirrup when standing on ground level with him, she can either find some spot on which to stand which will put her on a higher level than her horse, or she can lengthen her stirrup and shorten it again when mounted.

To describe the procedure in detail:

1. The rider stands with her back to her horse's head and takes her reins and whip in her left hand and her stirrup in her right. Her left hand on the bottom pommel gives her support while she puts her left foot into the stirrup.
2. She then moves her left hand on to the top pommel while grasping the leaping head with her right hand, and springs up till she has got her weight in her stirrup and the outside of her knee against the saddle, with her body still facing the horse's tail.
3. Catching hold of the back of her saddle with her right hand,

she continues to get up; and, *while levering her foot away from her horse's side by pressing her knee against the saddle* and pivoting on it, she turns to the left, puts her right leg over to the off-side, and sits down on the saddle as though riding astride.

4. She can then steady herself with her right hand on the top pommel, or, if she likes, with her left hand on the leaping head, while she brings her right leg over the horse's withers into position.

Her skirt need not interfere in any way if it is gathered together and made to hang across her left thigh and down her left side as she starts to mount.

The levering of the foot away from the horse's side described in (3), above, is important, as this ensures that the toe does not touch the horse's side and make him move away. The secret lies in keeping the back facing the horse's head until the whole of the weight is in the stirrup, when the rider will find that she can use her knee against the saddle to keep her toe away. Not till then should she begin to turn towards the saddle. If she watches this point carefully, and also, when in the saddle, never allows her horse to move till she indicates her wish for him to do so, he will soon learn to stand perfectly still while she is mounting. This good habit, however, will very soon be broken if she pokes him with her toe when mounting, or allows him to move of his own accord directly she is sitting in the saddle.

Many women like to be given what is called a "leg up". This can be neat, quick, and graceful, but it necessitates the presence of another person. The rider stands facing her horse's head with the reins and whip in her right hand and with both hands on the top pommel. She bends her left knee, and her assistant takes her foot in both hands. "One, two, three", and on the word "three" the rider springs and straightens her left leg while her assistant holds his hands firm, but does not attempt to lift her until her leg is straight. As she springs she turns to the left and sits sideways

APPENDIX I

on her saddle behind her pommels. She can now put her right leg forward into position.

To dismount, the rider takes the elastic off her right foot, pulls her skirt back to the left, takes her reins and whip in her right hand, and brings her right leg back over her pommels, which she holds while sitting sideways behind them and sliding to the ground. She must be careful not to catch her skirt over the pommels.

APPENDIX II

Fitting of the Side-Saddle. Girths. Balance Strap. Shape of the Seat. Care of the Saddle

With the saddle placed on the horse's back so that it sits just behind the big muscle of his shoulder, the front arch should be well clear of the withers, and the stuffing of the pannels should nowhere touch the backbone. The pannels should lie evenly all along the back and also down to the point of the tree.

To examine the fit we should lift up the flap on the near side, slip our hand in underneath the saddle and run it right down to the point of the tree; then similarly pass our hand under the saddle on the off side.

If the tree is too narrow at the point, all the bearing on the near side will be found to come on that spot, and the saddle will be lifted right up out of the hollow behind the horse's shoulder. In this case a wider tree is required.

If, when we are mounted, we find that the saddle slips over to the near side, even though we are sitting in a balanced position, this may be due to insufficient stuffing, either on the off side, or on the left pannel, or at the point of the tree on the near side; or it may be due to the tree being altogether too wide. The first three faults can be corrected by more stuffing where required; the last, unless we wish to keep the saddle for use on horses very thick through the body, can also, possibly, be rectified with more

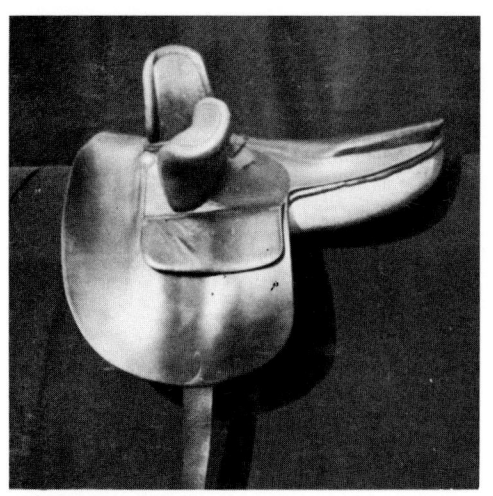

Plate 34 A WELL BALANCED SIDE-SADDLE
Showing the lower pommel in the "ordinary" position.

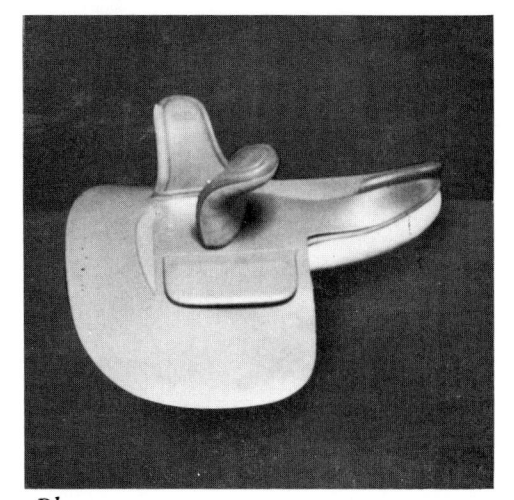

Plate 35 A WELL BALANCED SIDE-SADDLE
Showing the "Leaping Head" Pommel, which fulfils a "dual role", it is placed lower and further forward.

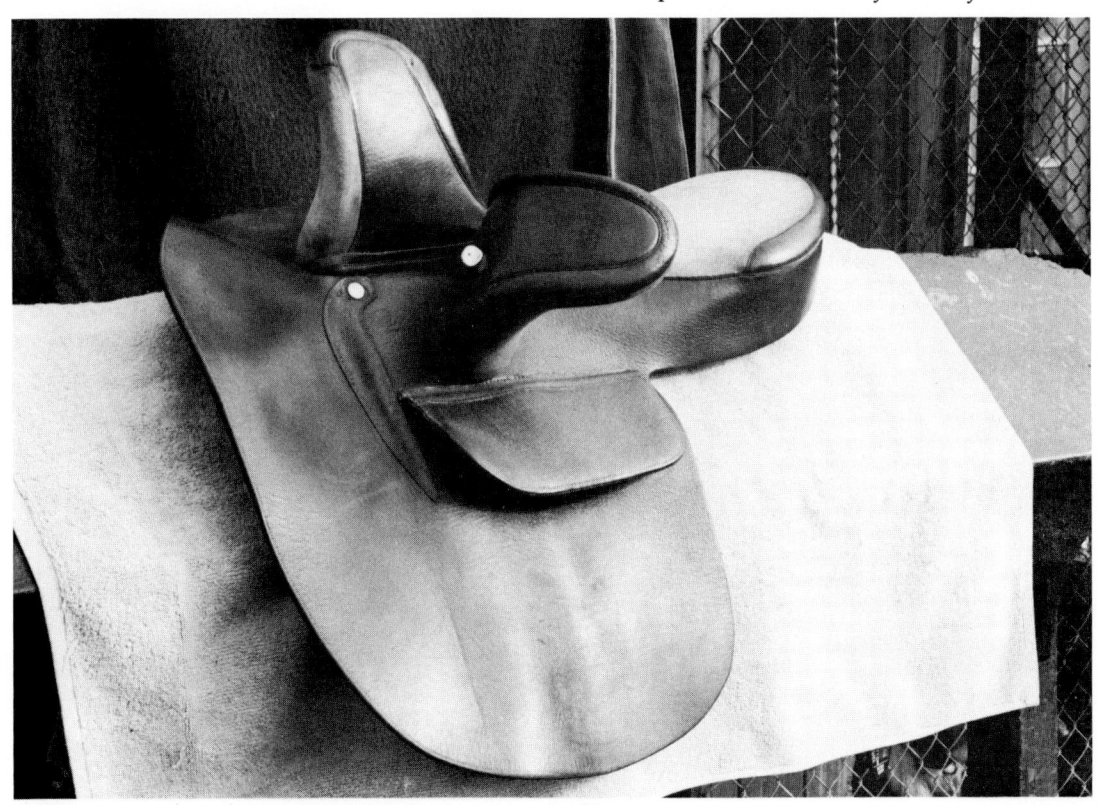

Plate 36 A STRIPPED SIDE-SADDLE (near-side)
A well balanced saddle ready to be stuffed.

Plate 37 A STRIPPED SIDE-SADDLE (off-side) *Showing how the girth is attached to the saddle. In this instance the balance strap is attached to the girth itself.*

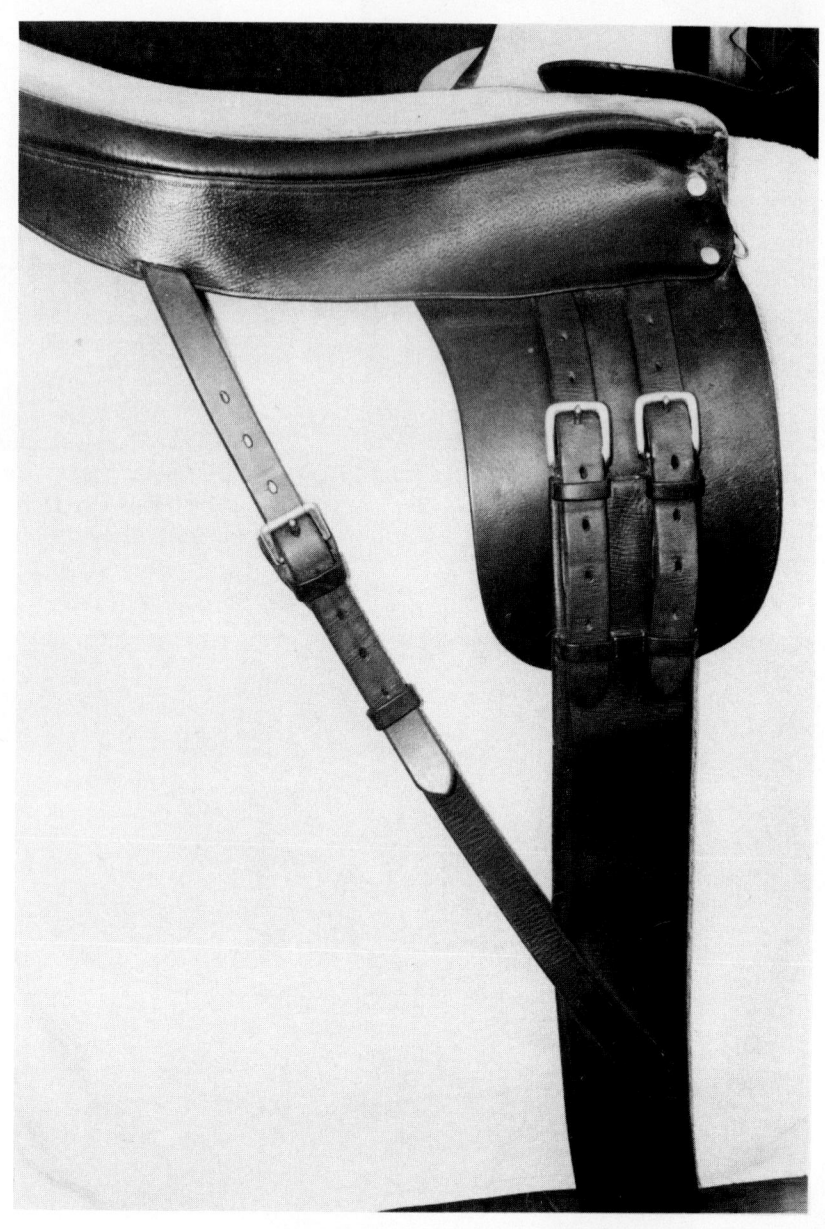

Opposite page

Plate 38 STIRRUP BAR (Mayhew pattern) *In the closed position.*

Plate 39 STIRRUP BAR (Mayhew pattern) *In open position.*

Plate 40 STIRRUP BAR (Mayhew pattern) *Closed, but with stirrup leather fitted.*

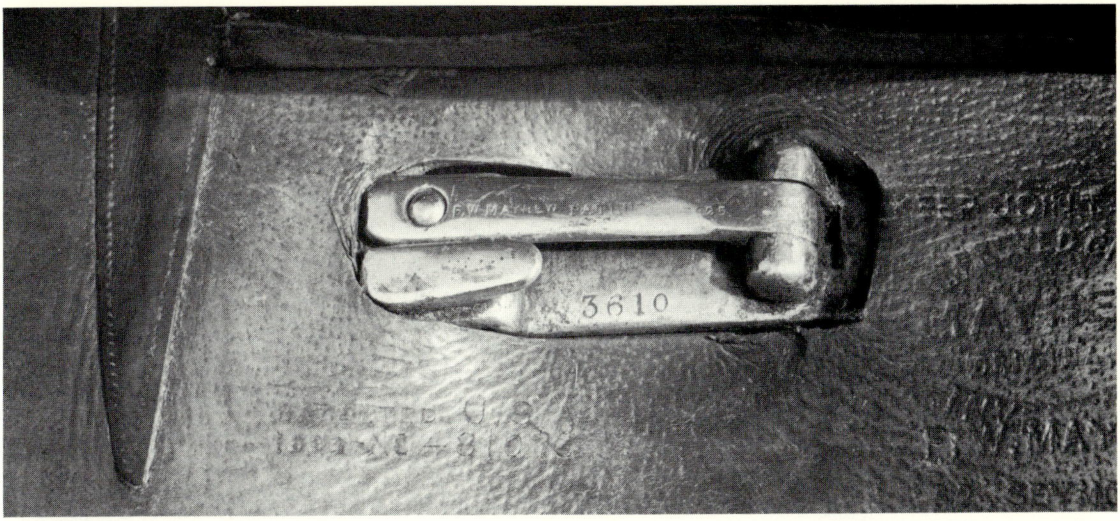
3610

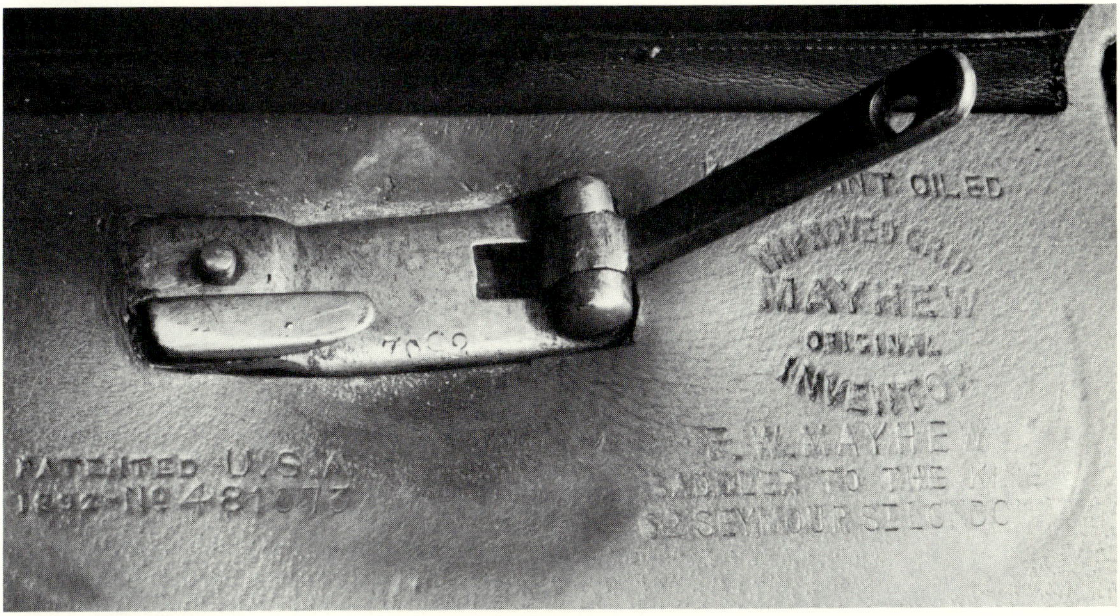
MAYHEW
PATENTED U.S.A

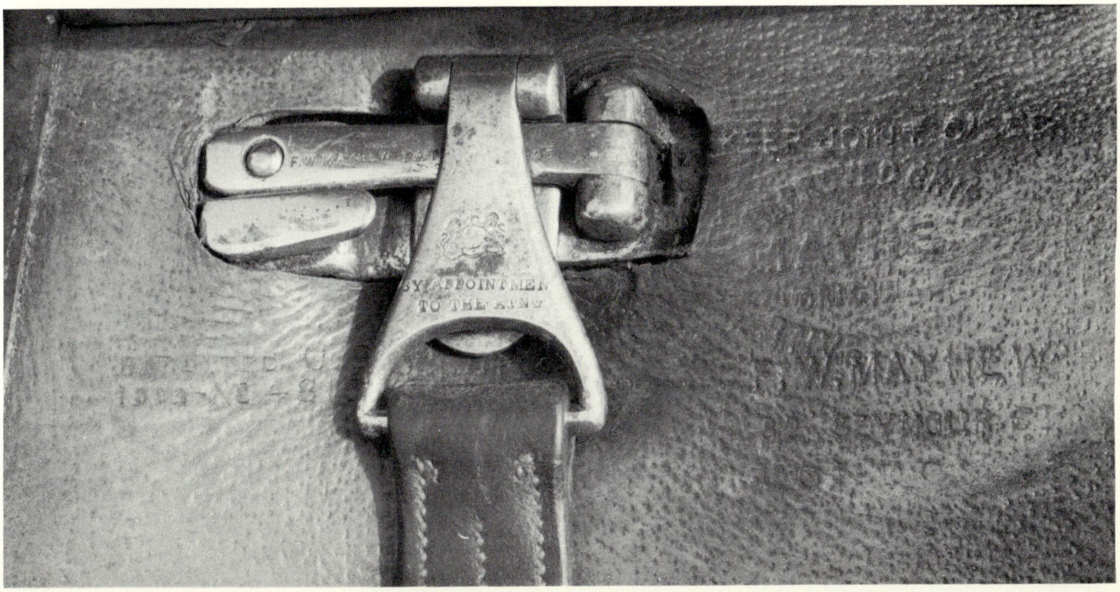
TO THE KING

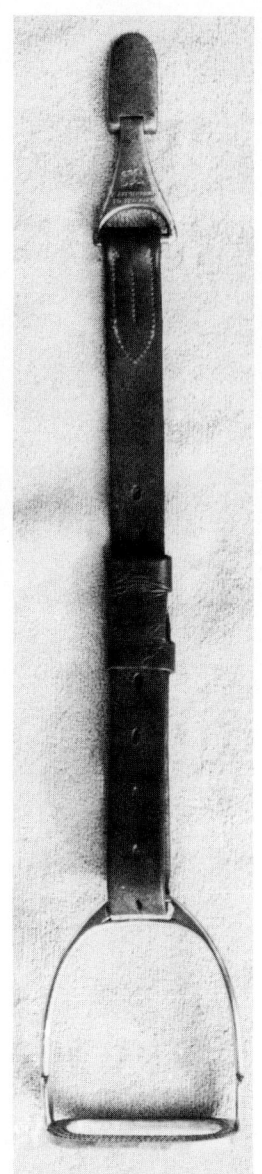

Plate 41 STIRRUP IRON
AND LEATHER
Mayhew attachment.

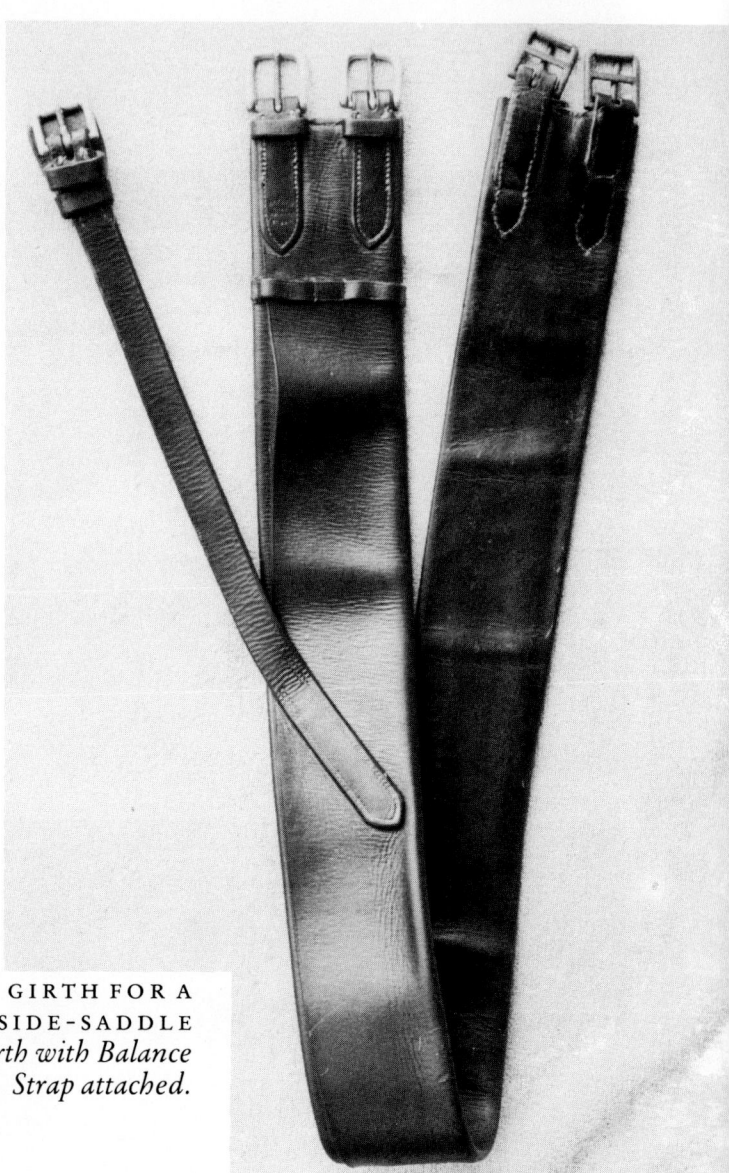

Plate 42 GIRTH FOR A
SIDE-SADDLE
*Leather girth with Balance
Strap attached.*

APPENDIX II

stuffing; but this is generally unsatisfactory, and a saddle with a narrower tree is really required.

The girth should not be drawn so tight that it causes discomfort to the horse. If he has a reasonably good shoulder, a very tight girth is quite unnecessary.

The wearing of a balance strap is entirely a matter of individual taste, but if it is used it should not be pulled up tight enough to cause the horse discomfort.

In an old-fashioned dipped seat it is difficult and tiring to keep the weight poised far enough forward; on the other hand, a completely straight seat is considered by many to go to the opposite extreme and to tip the rider forward too far. The usual practice today is to build saddles with approximately a quarter-inch (6 mm) dip, and this seems to strike the happy mean and to be comfortable to most women.

Few people realise how easily the tree of a side-saddle can be broken, and few grooms are sufficiently careful. Besides the most obvious cause – *i.e.*, a horse falling and rolling on his saddle – the following incidents often cause broken trees:

1. A fall from a height. Saddles should never be balanced on the top of the door (one sees this being done time and time again) or on any other support on which the saddle does not sit really firmly. Neither should a saddle be left on a horse without having the girth done up or someone present to hold it, as he can so easily shake it off or dislodge it by turning sharply round. It may be that a girth does not fit, another has to be fetched, the horse shakes, and crash – the saddle is on the ground.
2. Being rolled on. A horse should never be left with a saddle on his back unless he is tied up so that he cannot get down to roll. On a horse's return from work, many grooms will leave him with his saddle on his back, perhaps only for the time it takes to put his bridle in the cleaning-room, but during

those few seconds the horse may roll and the damage be done.
3. Being tightly girthed on a horse standing in a stall or narrow box *before* he has been turned round. Such a sharp turn causes great expansion of the horse's muscles under the tree, and will spread or break it if the saddle is girthed up.
4. Being used on a horse that is too wide for the tree, especially if used for jumping; this may also either stretch or break the tree.

APPENDIX III

Suppling Exercises

Exercises will be found to be a great help in developing a firm yet supple seat. They should be practised mounted, first when standing still and then on the move. The following is a good representative selection:

1. *Head Rolling.* Hold the shoulders erect and steady, but not stiff, and make the top of the head describe the largest possible circle, first in one direction and then in the other.

2. *Arm Swinging.* Keeping the shoulders erect and level:
   (a) Swing the arms like a pendulum, backwards as far as they will go and forwards to the horizontal position. This should be done with one arm at a time and then with both arms together, but working in opposite directions. This, besides being a suppling exercise, when done on the move helps to develop a sense of rhythm.
   (b) Let the arms, separately and then together, describe a complete circle with a really vigorous swing.

3. *Trunk turning.*
   (a) Place the right hand on the horse's near shoulder, and the left hand, behind the body, on his off hip, and then swing forward and round to the right, moving the left hand to the horse's off shoulder and the right hand to his

near hip. Continue to swing briskly from one position to the other.

(*b*) With the head and shoulders erect and the arms held out horizontally and in a direct line with each other, swing the body round from one side to the other as far as it will go.

4. *Body Bending*. Bend the body forward from below the hip as far as it will go, keeping the whole spine in the same vertical plane as that of the horse.

While doing all the above exercises the seat should remain still on the saddle, and no movement should be allowed below the point where the legs join the body.

5. *Leg Swinging*. Take the foot out of the stirrup, and, with the knee and thigh lying perfectly still on the saddle in their normal position, swing the leg, below the knee, backwards and forwards as far as it will go. Do not let it touch the horse's side, and keep the heel down throughout.

6. *Ankle Rolling*. Take the foot out of the stirrup. Keep the leg, as far down as the ankle, in its normal position and rotate the foot so that the toe describes the largest possible circle, first turning it several times in one direction and then in the other.

To help in getting the loins to work freely so that the seat remains on the saddle, put a handkerchief under the right seatbone, and endeavour to keep it there at walk, trot, and canter. This has an amazing psychological effect.

To keep the knee on the saddle, a handkerchief placed under the knee will have the same effect.

A stiff jaw generally indicates a tense body and possibly also a tense mind. If we loosen our jaw, it seems to have a relaxing effect on both. Therefore to chatter glibly when riding sometimes has its uses! So, too, when jumping, it is an excellent exercise to promote freedom and flexibility in our movements if we quote poetry or make any remark that strikes our fancy while we sail through the air!